The Organisation for Economic Cooperation and Development (OECD)

Celebrating its 60th anniversary in 2021, the Organisation for Economic Cooperation and Development (OECD) is routinely heralded as one of the leading organs of global governance, yet it remains one of the least written about and least well understood of our major global institutions.

This fully revised and updated second edition builds a well-rounded understanding of this crucial, though often neglected, institution. A range of clearly written chapters chart the origins and evolution of the organization, comprehend its influence, examine its current agenda, and evaluate its future prospects. Rather than the simplified characterizations of the OECD as a "rich-country's club" or "think tank," this book suggests that truly understanding the OECD and its significance to global governance requires it to be conceived as the entity it truly is: an international organization.

New to this edition:

- Outlines the OECD's origins and evolution, bringing its story fully up to date
- Considers the "OECD way" of working, including the peer review process
- Examines competing views of the OECD's influence over global governance
- Evaluates OECD reform and the organization's future prospects

This concise introduction continues to be vital reading for all students of international relations, politics and world history and affairs.

Richard Woodward is Assistant Lecturer in Business at Technological University Dublin. He has written extensively on different facets of the OECD and its contribution to global governance. His other research interests include soft power, tax havens, and development in small states.

Global Institutions

Edited by Thomas G. Weiss, *The CUNY Graduate Center, New York, USA* and Rorden Wilkinson, *University of New South Wales, Sydney, Australia*

About the series

The "Global Institutions Series" provides cutting-edge books about many aspects of what we know as "global governance." It emerges from our shared frustrations with the state of available knowledge—electronic and print-wise—for research and teaching. The series is designed as a resource for those interested in exploring issues of international organization and global governance. And since the first volumes appeared in 2005, we have taken significant strides toward filling many conceptual gaps.

The books in the series also provide a segue to the foundation volume that offers the most comprehensive textbook treatment available dealing with all the major issues, approaches, institutions, and actors in contemporary global governance. The second edition of our edited work *International Organization and Global Governance* (2018) contains essays by many of the authors in the series.

Understanding global governance—past, present, and future—is far from a finished journey. The books in this series nonetheless represent significant steps toward a better way of conceiving contemporary problems and issues as well as, hopefully, doing something to improve world order. We value the feedback from our readers and their role in helping shape the on-going development of the series.

A complete list of titles can be viewed online here: https://www.routledge.com/Global-Institutions/book-series/GI.

Small Countries, Big Diplomacy
Laos in the UN, ASEAN and MRC
Alounkeo Kittikhoun and Anoulak Kittikhoun

Global Climate and Energy Governance
Towards an Integrated Architecture
Harald L. Heubaum

The Organisation for Economic Cooperation and Development (OECD)

Second edition

Richard Woodward

Routledge
Taylor & Francis Group
LONDON AND NEW YORK

Second edition published 2022
by Routledge
4 Park Square, Milton Park, Abingdon, Oxon, OX14 4RN

and by Routledge
605 Third Avenue, New York, NY 10158

Routledge is an imprint of the Taylor & Francis Group, an informa business

First edition published by Routledge 2009

British Library Cataloguing-in-Publication Data
A catalogue record for this book is available from the British Library

Library of Congress Cataloging-in-Publication Data
Names: Woodward, Richard, 1976-, author.
Title: The organisation for economic cooperation and development (OECD) / Richard Woodward.
Description: 2nd edition. | Milton Park, Abingdon, Oxon; New York: Routledge, 2022. | Series: Global institutions | Includes bibliographical references and index.
Identifiers: LCCN 2021049985 (print) | LCCN 2021049986 (ebook) | ISBN 9781138494701 (hardback) | ISBN 9781032227443 (paperback) | ISBN 9781351025867 (ebook)
Subjects: LCSH: Organisation for Economic Co-operation and Development.
Classification: LCC HC241 .W66 2022 (print) | LCC HC241 (ebook) | DDC 338.9--dc23/eng/20211014
LC record available at https://lccn.loc.gov/2021049985
LC ebook record available at https://lccn.loc.gov/2021049986

ISBN: 9781138494701 (hbk)
ISBN: 9781032227443 (pbk)
ISBN: 9781351025867 (ebk)

DOI: 10.4324/9781351025867

Typeset in Times New Roman
by KnowledgeWorks Global Ltd.

Contents

List of illustrations

Tables

Figures

Box

Abbreviations

AEOI	Automatic Exchange of Information
AI	Artificial Intelligence
AIIB	Asian Infrastructure Investment Bank
BEPS	Base Erosion and Profit Shifting
BIAC	Business and Industry Advisory Committee
BIS	Bank for International Settlements
BRICS	Brazil, Russia, India, China, South Africa
CCNM	OECD Centre for Cooperation with Non-Members
CCXG	Climate Change Expert Group
CEEC	Committee on European Economic Cooperation
CERI	OECD Centre for Educational Research and Innovation
CFC	Chlorofluorocarbons
CSO	Civil Society Organizations
DAC	OECD Development Assistance Committee
DAG	OECD Development Assistance Group
DCD	OECD Development Cooperation Directorate
DELSA	Directorate for Employment, Labour and Social Affairs
ECO	OECD Economics Department
EDRC	OECD Economic and Development Review Committee
EC	European Community
EEC	European Economic Community
EFTA	European Free Trade Association
EMEF	Emerging Market Economy Forum
EPC	OECD Economic Policy Committee
EPU	European Payments Union
EU	European Union
FAO	Food and Agriculture Organization
FATF	Financial Action Task Force
FSF	Financial Stability Forum
GATT	General Agreement on Tariffs and Trade

GNI	Gross National Income
GNP	Gross National Product
GPEDC	Global Partnership for Effective Development Cooperation
GVC	Global Value Chain
G7	Group of Seven
G8	Group of Eight
G20	Group of Twenty
HLM	(DAC) High Level Meeting
ICT	Information and Communication Technology
IEA	International Energy Agency
ILO	International Labour Organization
IMF	International Monetary Fund
LIEO	Liberal International Economic Order
MAD	Decision of the Council concerning the Mutual Acceptance of Data in the Assessment of Chemicals
MAI	Multilateral Agreement on Investment
MCM	OECD Ministerial Council Meeting
MDG	Millennium Development Goals
MLI	Multilateral Convention to Implement Tax Treaty Related Measures to Prevent Base Erosion and Profit Shifting
NAEC	New Approaches to Economic Challenges
NATO	North Atlantic Treaty Organization
NGO	Non-Governmental Organization
NIEO	New International Economic Order
OAPEC	Organization of Arab Petroleum Exporting Countries
ODA	Official Development Assistance
OECD	Organization for Economic Co-operation and Development
OEEC	Organization for European Economic Co-operation
OLIS	Online Information System
OPEC	Organization of the Petroleum Exporting Countries
PAC	OECD Public Affairs and Communications Directorate
PIAAC	Programme for the International Assessment of Adult Competencies
PISA	Programme for International Student Assessment
PISA-D	PISA for Development
PSI	Private Sector Instruments
PWB	Programme of Work and Budget
QMV	Qualified Majority Voting
SDG	Sustainable Development Goals
SEC	Special Economic Committee

SME	Small and Medium size Enterprises
STI	OECD Directorate for Science, Technology and Innovation
STRI	Services Trade Restrictiveness Index
TiVA	Trade in Value Added
TSE	Total Support Estimate
TUAC	Trade Union Advisory Committee
UN	United Nations
UNCTAD	United Nations Conference on Trade and Development
UNDP	United Nations Development Programme
UNEP	United Nations Environment Programme
UNESCO	United Nations Educational, Scientific and Cultural Organization
UNFCCC	United Nations Framework Convention on Climate Change
WHO	World Health Organization
WISE	Centre on Well-being, Inclusion, Sustainability and Equal Opportunity
WP3	OECD Working Party Number 3 on Policies for the Promotion of Better International Payments Equilibrium
WTO	World Trade Organization

Foreword

In the twelve years that have elapsed since the first edition of this book was written research into the OECD has, like the organization and the world it inhabits, undergone drastic change. Back then the OECD was something of an enigma, arguably the least written about and least well understood of our major global institutions. Indeed, undertaking research into the OECD was a lonely occupation. Seldom were fellow OECD travelers encountered and, when they were, it was an article of faith that they would be grappling with problems more appalling and impassable than your own. More time was expended grumbling about accessing information about the OECD than discussing the merits of our respective academic contributions. Accordingly, the original version of this book, as well as setting out to fill a significant gap in the global governance literature, was something of a ground clearing exercise designed to open up the debate on a long neglected institution. Happily, in the intervening period, scholars have taken up this challenge with gusto. More books on the OEEC/OECD were published in the 2010s than in the previous six decades combined and articles about the organization's role in global governance appeared more frequently in leading international journals. This work, much of it based on material excavated from the OECD archives or fresh interviews with key players, has filled out the historical record and injected additional nuance into the theories and frameworks which seek to explain the organization's influence.

Paradoxically, this belated interest in the OECD has coincided with an era where the institution's future, and that of the liberal international order, is in question. The first edition of the book ended on a cautiously optimistic note, suggesting that if the OECD could manage the tensions inherent in its reform process "the heyday of this enigmatic organization may yet be to come." In many respects, the reforms instigated during Angel Gurria's tenure as Secretary-General were successful. By fortifying its portfolio of non-member partnerships, especially with the rising powers of the Global South and the G20, the OECD has globalized its role and the recognition of its standards. This has translated into a higher public profile for the organization and bolstered its relevance to existing members. Furthermore, with eight new members joining since 2010 and half a dozen applications under consideration, it is likely that by the end of the next decade the OECD will have doubled in size since the end of the Cold War. Many members, however, worry that the growth of the OECD and its entanglements with non-members are fundamentally altering the organization's identity and character. As such, the pace of the reform process has dwindled. Worse, reforms at the OECD are being outpaced by changes in the global political system. Despite expansion, the OECD's collective weight in the global economy continues to shrink intensifying doubts about the legitimacy and efficacy of the organization as a venue in which to pursue the problems of global governance. Instilling a clear vision for the organization that commands the support of OECD members, yet befits changing geopolitical circumstances, is an urgent challenge facing Mathias Cormann, the new OECD Secretary-General from June 2021.

In the writing of this book, there are a number of people to whom I am indebted. First, I would like to thank Rorden Wilkinson, Thomas Weiss and Filippos Pierros, the former Deputy Permanent Representative of the EU to the OECD, for their thorough and perceptive feedback on earlier versions of the manuscript and their forbearance in the delays to its arrival. My gratitude is also due to Jan-Anno Schuur, Aurelia Radu, Marie-Ange Sicaire and Ruud Bruijns, the OECD librarians and archivists who answered my queries promptly and diligently, kept me going through long hours sat at a microfiche reader and provided excellent advice on the OECD's catering facilities! I have had many stimulating conversations about the OECD with current and former members of staff, most notably William Hynes, Simon Scott, Richard Carey and Alexandra Trzeciak-Duval. Thanks are also due to the growing regiment of scholars engaged in OECD research whose wisdom and insights inform what follows: Ruth Ben-Artzi, Samuel Beroud, Peter Carroll, Judith Clifton, Alison Christians, Richard Eccleston, Katrin Eggenberger, Anja Jakobi, Aynsley Kellow, Bob Kurdle, Matthieu Leimgruber, Rianne Mahon, Kerstin Martens, Stephen McBride, Stephanie McLeod, Tony Porter, and Matthias Schmelzer. My greatest debt of all, however, is to my wife, Lucy, whose patience, perspective and love makes my world a better place.

Introduction

On 30 September 1961, the Convention on the Organisation for Economic Cooperation and Development (OECD) came into force giving birth to what is now a 38 member "forum in which governments work together to seek solutions to common problems, share experiences, and identify best practices to promote policies for better lives."[1] Despite its unprepossessing temperament, the fingerprints of the OECD and its forerunner, the Organisation for European Economic Cooperation (OEEC), are etched on many defining moments of post-war economic history including the administration of the Marshall Plan (1948–51), the resolution of the oil crises (1973), the completion of the Uruguay Round trade negotiations (1986–94), the genesis of the Millennium Development Goals (MDGs), and the response to the Global Financial Crisis (2008). From the definition of Official Development Assistance (ODA) and the principle that the polluter pays to standards for national income accounting and guidelines governing the collection of personal data, these organizations have also been a crucible in which a medley of ideas, discourses, concepts, practices, and rules that underpin global governance crystallized.

Unsurprisingly, the OECD is routinely heralded as a leading organ of global governance, yet it is only recently that the organization's role and influence has received any sustained scholarly treatment.[2] Nevertheless, most surveys of international organizations and global governance consign the OECD to the sidelines or resort to crude and sometimes misleading soubriquets to describe it. For example, pundits habitually refer to the OECD as a "developed" or "rich country's club"[3]. Collectively, OECD members have always accounted for three-fifths to four-fifths of global Gross National Income (GNI) in dollar terms (see Table 2.1), but the accuracy of this label is betrayed by the persistent exclusion of some wealthy countries from the OECD and widespread variation in its member's economic and human development (see Table I.1).

DOI: 10.4324/9781351025867-1

Table I.1 Members of the OECD - key indicators

Member State	Year of Accession	GNP per capita 1963 (US$ PPP)	GDP per capita 2019 (US$ PPP)	GDP per capita Rank 2019	GDP 2019 (US$ bn PPP)	GDP Rank 2019	Human Development Index Rank 2020
Canada	1961	2,263	51,342	21	1,929	16	16
United States	1961	3,090	65,298	8	21,427	2	17
United Kingdom	1961	1,564	48,698	24	3,255	9	13
Denmark	1961	1,700	60,179	11	348	52	10
Iceland	1961	1,440*	60,061	12	21	142	4
Norway	1961	1,537	66,832	7	357	51	1
Turkey	1961	230	28,134	52	2,325	13	54
Spain	1961	220#	42,195	32	1,987	15	25
Portugal	1961	304	36,639	39	374	50	38
France	1961	1,671	49,435	22	3,315	8	26
Ireland	1961	757	88,241	4	436	47	2=
Belgium	1961	1,500	54,905	17	626	34	14
Greece	1961	464	30,722	46	336	53	32
Germany	1961	1,641†	56,278	15	4,659	5	6
Switzerland	1961	2,010	70,989	5	608	36	2=
Sweden	1961	2,045	55,820	16	574	38	7
Austria	1961	1,076	58,946	14	524	40	18
Netherlands	1961	1,212	59,554	13	1034	25	8
Luxembourg	1961	1,606	121,293	1	75	101	23
Italy	1962	899	44,248	27	2,664	11	29
Japan	1964	620	43,236	30	5,459	4	19
Finland	1969	-	51,426	20	283	58	11
Australia	1971	-	53,469	18	1,352	18	8
New Zealand	1973	-	43,953	28	216	65	14
Mexico	1994	-	20,582	64	2,603	12	74
Czech Republic	1995	-	43,300	29	454	45	27
Hungary	1996	-	34,507	40	331	54	40
Poland	1996	-	34,431	41	1,299	20	35
South Korea	1996	-	43,142	31	2,224	14	23
Slovak Republic	2000	-	34,067	42	186	69	39
Chile	2010	-	25,155	56	476	43	43
Slovenia	2010	-	40,983	35	84	96	22
Israel	2010	-	42,146	33	381	49	19
Estonia	2010	-	38,915	36	51	110	29
Latvia	2016	-	32,191	45	61	103	37
Lithuania	2018	-	38,502	38	111	83	34
Colombia	2020		15,635	83	787	31	83
Costa Rica	2021		21,738	63	110	84	62

* Figures for 1960.
\# Figures for 1962.
† The 1963 figure is for the Federal Republic of Germany only.

Sources: OECD, "The OECD Member Countries," *OECD Observer* 13 (December 1964): 21-22; World Bank World Development Indicators, https://databank.worldbank.org/source/world-development-indicators; UNDP, *Human Development Report 2020*, http://www.hdr.undp.org/

At the outset, the per capita incomes of the poorest members were one-sixth of the OECD mean. Moving to the present of the 83 territories classified by the World Bank in 2021 as "high income economies,"[4] 49 were not members of the organization. Conversely, Mexico, Turkey and Colombia are OECD members but are not categorized as high-income economies and languish behind many non-member economies in the United Nations Development Programme's (UNDP's) Human Development Index.[5] Elsewhere the OECD has been pigeon-holed as a "think tank,"[6] "consultative forum,"[7] and a "pool of statistical and economic expertise."[8] These epithets each illuminate elements of the OECD but cast others into darkness. This book suggests that providing a panoramic perspective on the OECD requires it to be described and analyzed it as the entity it truly is: an international organization.

International organizations and global governance: The case of the OECD

Since the term was first coined in the 1990s, global governance has become ubiquitous in the academic and policymaking lexicon. The gigantic literature that appeared in the interim refined the concept; ultimately, however, commentators cleave closely to the idea that global governance is "the sum of the informal and formal ideas, values, norms, procedures, and institutions that help all actors……identify, understand and address trans-boundary problems."[9] Despite the possibility of "governance without government,"[10] most reviews of global governance subscribe to the view that states, albeit in conjunction with a bevy of other actors, remain the preeminent repositories of power and authority in world politics and, hence, the primary managers of humankind's common affairs.[11] The mismatch between the territorially bounded power of states and the worldwide scale of the common affairs they crave to manage is a central conundrum of global governance. Loath to surrender sovereignty to supranational organizations, states have resorted to a labyrinth of mechanisms to facilitate international cooperation, the most conspicuous of which are international organizations, "formal, continuous structures founded by an authoritative instrument of agreement between members (including two or more sovereign states) or an existing international organization through which members pursue their common interests."[12]

Attempts to delineate the OECD's influence on global governance are muddied by imprecision in the OECD Convention and contrasting theoretical convictions about the properties of international organizations.

Article 1 of the OECD Convention[13] states the aims of the organization shall be to "promote policies" designed:

a to achieve the highest sustainable economic growth and employment and a rising standard of living in Member countries, while maintaining financial stability, and thus to contribute to the development of the world economy;
b to contribute to sound economic expansion in Member as well as non-member countries in the process of economic development; and
c to contribute to the expansion of world trade on a multilateral, non-discriminatory basis in accordance with international obligations.

The OECD was to prosecute this mission by institutionalizing cooperation between the members and, where appropriate, between member and non-member states. To this end, Article 3 commits signatories to:

a keep each other informed and furnish the Organisation with the information necessary for the accomplishment of its tasks;
b consult together on a continuing basis, carry out studies and participate in agreed projects; and
c co-operate closely and where appropriate take co-ordinated action.

This apparently straightforward set of objectives (promoting sustainable economic growth and development, maximizing employment and living standards, and nurturing the global trade regime) and means of their pursuit (cooperative endeavors between states) masks the ambivalence surrounding the OECD's role. Delivering on blanket goals such as the promotion of economic growth and living standards has necessitated the OECD's colonization of almost every facet of social and economic life, turning it into a "restricted forum for virtually unrestricted topics."[14] Equally because the convention confers responsibilities that overlap with other major agencies of global governance, the OECD is vulnerable to forum shopping. The result is an elastic organization whose functional domain is in perpetual flux. Likewise, Article 3 makes the delivery of the OECD's mandate reliant on something that states are not always predisposed to do: cooperate. International cooperation is inhibited by uncertainties about the essence of the problems at hand, the preferences of others, the merits of different solutions, and fears that partners will defect from agreements in order to steal a march on their rivals. Thus, the convention is a useful starting point but leaves unanswered questions about what issues arise in the OECD, how the OECD assists in their resolution, and whether and why the OECD's activities exert influence over global governance.

There is widespread agreement about the functions the OECD performs and the organization's way of working (see Figure 3.5). As well as collecting data, analyzing policy and undertaking economic surveillance, the OECD offers a platform where senior policy makers can engage in continuous dialogue about contemporary issues, exchange best practices, review each other's policies, evolve norms and standards and, sporadically, develop and negotiate agreements.[15] Where analyses of the OECD diverge is in their interpretation of the implications of these activities for global governance.

For many years, insights about the OECD's role in global governance came courtesy of rationalist theories of international relations that perceive international organizations as "empty shells or impersonal policy machinery to be manipulated by other actors."[16] From this standpoint, the OECD was a mere arena in which states interact to forge common goals and strive for multilateral agreements that serve their preordained interests. By providing states with better information, interactions at the OECD decreased the aforementioned misgivings surrounding international cooperation. Through the OECD's statistics and analysis and the ongoing exchange of policy knowledge, experience and ideas in OECD meetings, states come to learn about the preferences of their counterparts and are socialized into shared beliefs about the problems they face and the best ways of settling them. Consensus about the substance of the issues is a prerequisite for the development of legal instruments solemnized at the OECD Council that constrain state behavior. As Chapter 3 discusses, seldom is the OECD used as a framework for reaching formal agreements. When it is, agreements overwhelmingly take the form of "soft law" entailing loose obligations to enact indeterminate best practices. The OECD's peer reviews and surveillance would reveal non-compliance but, because the Convention did not invest the organization with material resources to discipline states, are considered toothless. This research therefore concludes that the OECD has a negligible impact on the trajectory of global governance. At most, the OECD is a weathervane whose disposition and direction are determined by the gusts generated from the clashing interests of powerful states.

Modern writing on the OECD shows that rationalist approaches offer a fragmentary picture that understates the organization's influence.

By fixating on the OECD's ability to help states manage their interdependence through attaining and policing legal agreements, rationalists look only at the tip of the OECD iceberg. Many of the areas under the OECD's purview (see Chapter 5), "do not involve the interdependence that characterizes most issues on which states collaborate."[17] Similarly, despite the rarity of codified accords and the absence of rewards and sanctions, it is difficult to sustain the argument that the OECD was impotent. Rationalist accounts struggled to account for the regularity with which the OECD's soft law was incorporated into "hard" treaties established in universal international organizations (see Chapters 1 and 2), the OECD's findings and instruments were invoked by policymakers and civil society groups to justify or critique policy stances, members adopted the OECD's best practices, and why topics ostensibly unconnected with the interests of leading members became embedded into the OECD's agenda. To make sense of this, most contemporary academic commentary on the OECD supplements the rationalist worldview with constructivist theories that acknowledge "even when they lack material resources, IOs exercise power as they constitute and construct the world."[18]

Instead of eyeing it as the aggregation or creature of state interests, constructivist narratives proceed from the premise that the OECD is a purposive actor capable of pushing its own agendas. The OECD's importance to global governance inheres not in the production and enforcement of legal texts but in producing and diffusing knowledge and ideas that influence the interests, identities and behaviour of states. The slack in the Convention was arguably a deliberate ploy by its creators to imbue the organization with the autonomy to carry out its role and the agility to respond to new contingencies but also opened up the possibility for the OECD to act independently. To be clear, the argument is not that the OECD pursues agendas antithetical to the interests of member states (although such pathologies are possible[19]), but it can orient states toward particular problems, ways of perceiving them and potential solutions. Flipping the rationalist logic on its head, the constructivists suggest that rather than always dictating what topics the OECD should cover on the basis of their interests, states *learn* from the OECD about the topics they have an interest in tackling.

To do this, the OECD relies on the authority arising from its expertise. The OECD secretariat (see Chapter 3) contains highly educated individuals possessing specialist scientific knowledge. Such perspicacity coaxes "us to confer on experts, and the bureaucracies that house them, the authority to make judgements and solve problems."[20] The OECD's expert status allows it to transform issues or events into governable problems, propagate ideas and policy agendas, and endorse norms and best practices. Through meetings at the OECD participants learn about each other and their place in the world and are socialized into "global knowledge networks"[21] or "epistemic communities"[22] sharing common mindsets or understandings of policy issues. As with the rationalists, learning and socialization are recognized as the key to construing the OECD's influence but for the constructivists the effects of these processes are more profound. Whereas the former see state interests as fixed or structurally determined, the latter contend that they are learnt through social interaction. Via contact with new ideas and opportunities for discursive interaction with representatives from the secretariat, member states, international organizations and civil society at the OECD states come to comprehend their interests differently. Over time these interactions also redefine the identities of the participants. The OECD is the "paradigmatic example of an identity-defining international organization.......it defines standards of appropriate behaviour for states that seek to identify themselves as modern, liberal, market-friendly and efficient."[23] States are predisposed to follow OECD norms and best practices not because they are mandatory but because they have been socialized into seeing these as appropriate standards of behavior for countries who are, or wish to be glimpsed as, members of the advanced international community. In short, rather than a weathervane buffeted by the unforgiving winds of power politics, the OECD is increasingly portrayed as a weather maker exerting an independent impact on global governance.

The book ahead

The first two chapters depict the OECD's history and its evolving role in global governance. Examining the period from 1948 to 1984, Chapter 1 sketches the OECD story from its roots in the European reconstruction process to the end of Emile van Lennep's tenure as Secretary-General. The OECD's origins lay in the Marshall Plan and the United States' insistence that recipient countries create a permanent organization to earmark this financial support. Besides allocating aid, the OEEC contributed significantly to the liberalization of Europe's trade and financial systems. By the end of the 1950s, the recovery of Western European economies meant the OEEC had outlived its original purpose. Disputes over European integration and the United States' demands that its allies assume more of the burden of international economic management sounded the OEEC's death knell. Equally, with Cold War antipathies rampant, the transatlantic community could see the virtue of retaining an organization through which they could manage their interdependence. The European designation was dropped, a development dimension added and the organization was reborn as the OECD. Over the next two decades, the OECD would become renowned for its expertise across an expanding universe of policy problems.

Chapter 2 considers the OECD's record from 1984 to the present. Despite retaining its fealty to markets, democracy and economic growth, in this era the OECD's character and bailiwick evolved markedly as it sought to cope with the geopolitical and ideational ferment of the post-Cold War world. Paradoxically, the apparent triumph of OECD values represented by the collapse of the communist bloc in Eastern Europe posed questions about the organization's relevance, especially given the growing weight of non-OECD states in the global economy. Compared with the Cold War period the OECD became more catholic, almost doubling its membership and canvassing greater inputs from non-members and civil society. The OECD also became an exponent of neoliberal economic models, something that shifted the organization's focus further in favor of finding the proper domestic policies as opposed to coordinating international macroeconomic policy.

Chapter 3 explores the OECD's organizational structure and decision-making procedures. Particular attention is paid to the tasks performed by the Secretary-General, the Council, the Secretariat, and the committee system and how they work together with member states (and a growing retinue of non-member states and civil society partners) to drive the OECD's work. Having thus considered the OECD's way of working, Chapter 4 reviews the literature concerning how and why this activity translates into influence in global governance. Chapter 5 outlines some of the contemporary issues that are under the OECD microscope. This account is not exhaustive but seeks to give the reader a feel for the richness of the organization's remit by touring the OECD's work in sustainable economic growth, trade, development, the environment, taxation, education, health, labor and social affairs, well-being, science, technology and digitalization.

With this range of analytical expertise allied to an enviable record of conceptual innovation and soothing tensions in the wider global governance infrastructure, the OECD's position ought to be impregnable. Alas, changing geopolitical realities and institutional competition cloud the OECD's outlook. Chapter 6 evaluates efforts under Secretary-General Angel Gurria to brighten the OECD's prospects through reforms encompassing membership enlargement, outreach to non-members and an informal role as secretariat to the Group of 20 (G20).

The reform package has shored up the OECD's immediate position but the member's disquiet about contradictions arising from the strategy, disagreement about the direction of further reform, and their dwindling faith in the value of multilateral cooperation mean questions about the organization's long-term future linger. Chapter 7 concludes the book by sketching three scenarios about the OECD's destiny. The first envisages the OECD's demise, its fate sealed by irrevocable changes in the pattern of global power. The second foresees the emergence of a successor organization in a world fragmenting into coexisting spheres of influence. The final scenario anticipates the OECD's survival, believing that it possesses the bureaucratic assets and institutional temperament to adjust to the currents of world politics and sustain its relevance to twenty-first century global governance.

Notes

1 OECD, *Secretary-General's Report to Ministers 2019* (Paris: OECD, 2019), 18.
2 Rianne Mahon and Stephen McBride, eds., *The OECD and Transnational Governance* (Vancouver: University of British Columbia Press, 2008); Kerstin Martens and Anja P. Jakobi, eds., *Mechanisms of OECD Governance: International Incentives for National Policy-Making* (Oxford: Oxford University Press, 2010); Peter Carroll and Aynsley Kellow, *The OECD: A Study of Organizational Adaptation* (Cheltenham: Edward Elgar, 2011); Matthias Schmelzer, *The Hegemony of Growth: The OECD and the Making of the Economic Growth Paradigm* (Cambridge: Cambridge University Press, 2016); Matthieu Leimgruber and Matthias Schmelzer, eds., *The OECD and the International Political Economy Since 1948* (Basingstoke: Palgrave, 2017).
3 Robert Gilpin, *The Challenge of Global Capitalism: The World Economy in the 21st Century* (Princeton, N.J.: Princeton University Press, 2000), 184.
4 World Bank, "World Bank Country and Lending Groups," https://datahelpdesk.worldbank.org/knowledgebase/articles/906519-world-bank-country-and-lending-groups.
5 UNDP, *World Development Report 2020: The Next Frontier Human Development and the Anthropocene* (New York: UNDP, 2020).
6 Philip Inman, "Governments should avoid Covid spending cuts and tax rises, says OECD," 16 September 2020 https://www.theguardian.com/business/2020/sep/16/governments-must-resist-covid-spending-cuts-and-tax-rises-says-oecd.
7 Henry G. Aubrey, *Atlantic Economic Cooperation: The Case of the OECD* (New York: Frederick A. Praeger, 1967), 102.
8 Scott Sullivan, *From War to Wealth: Fifty Years of Innovation* (Paris: OECD, 1997), 6.
9 Thomas G. Weiss and Rorden Wilkinson, "Rethinking Global Governance? Complexity, Authority, Power, Change," *International Studies Quarterly* 58, no. 1 (2014): 211.

10 James N. Rosenau and Ernst-Otto Czempiel, eds., *Governance Without Government: Order and Change in World Politics* (Cambridge: Cambridge University Press, 1992).
11 Richard Woodward, "Governance in a globalized world," in *The Handbook of Globalisation (3rd edition)*, ed. Jonathan Michie (Cheltenham: Edward Elgar, 2019), 326.
12 Michael Davies and Richard Woodward, *International Organizations: A Companion* (Cheltenham: Edward Elgar, 2014), 13.
13 OECD, "Convention on the Organisation for Economic Cooperation and Development," https://www.oecd.org/general/conventionontheorganisationforeconomicco-operationanddevelopment.htm.
14 James Salzman, "Labor Rights, Globalization and Institutions: The Role and Influence of the Organization for Economic Cooperation and Development," *Michigan Journal of International Law* 21, no. 4 (2000): 777.
15 David Henderson, "The Role of the OECD in Liberalising International Trade and Capital Flows," *The World Economy* 19, no. 1 (1996): 14; OECD, *The Contribution of International Organisations to a Rule-based International System* (Paris: OECD, 2019), 1.
16 Michael N. Barnett and Martha Finnemore, "The Politics, Power and Pathologies of International Organizations," *International Organization* 53, no. 4 (1999): 700.
17 Tony Porter and Michael Webb, "Role of the OECD in the Orchestration of Global Knowledge Networks," in *The OECD and Transnational Governance*, eds. Rianne Mahon and Stephen McBride (Vancouver: University of British Columbia Press, 2008), 43.
18 Barnett and Finnemore, "The Politics, Power and Pathologies of International Organizations," 700.
19 See, for example, David Howarth and Tal Sadeh, "In the vanguard of globalization: The OECD and international capital liberalization," *Review of International Political Economy* 18, no. 5 (2011): 622–45.
20 Michael Barnett and Martha Finnemore, *Rules for the World: International Organizations in Global Politics* (Ithaca, N.Y.: Cornell University Press, 2004), 24.
21 Tony Porter and Michael Webb, "Role of the OECD in the Orchestration of Global Knowledge Networks," 43–59.
22 Peter M. Haas, "Introduction: epistemic communities and international policy coordination," *International Organization* 46, no. 1 (1992): 1–35.
23 Tony Porter and Michael Webb, "Role of the OECD in the Orchestration of Global Knowledge Networks," 44.

1 The OECD's origins and early years

From reconstruction to renown

This chapter chronicles the OECD story from 1948 to 1984, teasing out the factors that compelled the organization's creation, drove its evolution, and impinged upon its role and performance in global governance. In many respects, the OECD saga is about the organization and its member's ongoing attempts to acclimatize to a world of their own making. Instilled with a liberalizing vocation the OECD, together with other multilateral institutions, was a key agent propelling international economic interdependence and devising rules to govern the consequences.

In the period covered by this chapter, four recurring and interrelated themes swayed the character and context of the OECD's operations. First, the OECD was an artifact of the patterns of material power in the global political system, most visibly US hegemony. In his closing address at the Bretton Woods Conference of 1944 Henry Morgenthau, US Treasury Secretary, said "we have come to recognize that the wisest and most effective way to protect our national interests is through international cooperation—that is to say, through united effort for the attainment of common goals."[1] To this end, the United States used its preponderant position to fashion a liberal international order, an assemblage of alliances, institutions and rules to govern the interactions among states, to which the OECD was integral.[2] The Western allies' post war economic recovery eroded US hegemony. The United States nevertheless remained pre-eminent and was a ubiquitous influence on the OECD's trajectory. Second, the OECD operated against the geopolitical backdrop of the Cold War. Starting as a transatlantic organization, the OECD grew to encompass all of the United States' major "Western" allies. As such, the OECD had a crucial role in constructing and constituting "the West" as an imagined community of states subscribing to the principle (though not always the practice) that capitalism and democracy surpassed authoritarianism

DOI: 10.4324/9781351025867-2

and central planning as organizing principles for global governance.[3] Besides providing an edifice in which the West could mollify tensions arising from their economic interdependence, the OECD also assisted the synchronization of their positions vis-à-vis the "rest," especially the communist bloc and later a bullish Global South.

Third, the OECD was preoccupied with the definition, measurement, and promotion of economic growth.[4] The search for policies to elevate economic growth impelled the OECD's expansion into areas, such as science and education, never envisaged in the Convention. As well as raising living standards, high rates of Western economic growth were imperative to winning the Cold War duel by bestowing the material power necessary to subdue to communist foe and signaling the virility of the capitalist system. Until the 1970s, the OECD's growth recipe echoed the "embedded liberal"[5] settlement augured at Bretton Woods with its advocacy of freer international markets countervailed by a commitment to Keynesian economic management which allowed states to appease domestic demands for social welfare and full employment. Subsequently, the Keynesian consensus was steadily eclipsed at the OECD by a neoliberal philosophy that encouraged states to embrace competition by eliminating remaining obstacles to commerce and capital. Finally, as a component in a wider circuitry of international policy-making, the OECD's fortunes were shaped by cooperation and competition with other multilateral economic institutions.

The remainder of the chapter is structured as follows. The next two sections consider the OEEC's origin, record and its metamorphosis into the OECD. Particular attention is paid to the United States' hegemonic influence in the conception and primitive development of these institutions. The third section scrutinizes the OECD under Thorkil Kristensen (1961–69). Acquiring a reputation for delineating concepts and providing impartial statistical analyses that helped states to define and map unexplored terrain, the OECD became intrinsic to the international regimes for trade, finance, and development. The OECD was also an antechamber where Western states coordinated their positions before they were accosted in the universal international organizations by numerically superior countries from the communist bloc and the Global South. The fourth section reflects on the reign of Emile van Lennep (1969–1984). A surreptitious salve for the economic convulsions that punctuated the 1970s, the OECD also finessed further rounds of international trade negotiations. Intensified institutional competition and signs of disenchantment among the members, manifested in the Group of 7's (G7's) entrance, were portents of impending problems, however. The conclusion recapitulates the chapter's key findings and summarizes the challenges facing the OECD as it entered the 1980s.

Reconstruction: The Organisation for European Economic Cooperation (OEEC) (1948–58)

The OECD story begins in the wake of the Second World War. Years of military conflict left the European economies prostrate. Their infrastructure and industrial capacity had been destroyed or remained on a war footing. Worse, the substantial sums spent prosecuting the war had drained European treasuries, hindering their reconstruction. Contrastingly, the US industrial base was unscathed and had boomed during the war. Accounting for two-thirds of global industrial output and with surplus capital to invest, the United States was the undisputed hegemon holding unrivalled power to configure the postwar world.

Anxious to avoid the mistakes made after the First World War and to counterbalance the communist threat posed by the USSR, the US administrations of Franklin Roosevelt and Harry Truman intervened. Between 1945 and 1947, the United States expended $9 billion to aid Europe's recovery. By mid-1947, it was apparent that this haphazard and bilateral approach was insufficient. Dwindling international liquidity had paralyzed intra-European trade, aggravating shortages of food, fuel, and raw materials. At this point, with several European economies verging on collapse, social unrest rampant, and communist parties making strides in France and Italy, the United States proffered a more comprehensive solution.

The Marshall Plan

In June 1947, Secretary of State George Marshall gestured the United States' willingness to lend the financial aid needed to salvage Europe's ailing economies through the European Recovery Program, known colloquially as the Marshall Plan. The caveat was that European states must cooperate to formulate and implement their own reconstruction blueprint. Beyond alleviating short-term humanitarian problems, the Marshall Plan served the United States' longer-term strategic interests. Specifically, it was an expression of the "containment" doctrine whereby the United States sought to stifle the spread of Soviet influence.[6] A cohesive, peaceful, and prosperous Europe was an indispensable bulwark against the USSR's expansive propensities. To this end, together with finance for reconstruction, the Marshall Plan aimed to enhance production and productivity, safeguard international financial stability, stimulate trade, and jumpstart European integration.

Fearing that the money might be squandered, the US Congress insisted on a continuing organization to oversee the Marshall Plan. The Soviet Union decided not to participate and denied its satellites a similar right and, in July 1947, 16 countries (Austria, Belgium, Denmark, France, Greece, Iceland, the Republic of Ireland, Italy, Luxembourg, the Netherlands, Norway, Portugal, Sweden, Switzerland, Turkey, and the United Kingdom) convened in Paris for the Conference on European Economic Cooperation. This meeting established a Committee on European Economic Cooperation (CEEC) and a coterie of technical committees to sketch the recovery program presented to the US government in September 1947. Following US backing for these proposals, the CEEC pondered the development of a permanent organization to administer it. These deliberations were marked by a schism between those, principally the United States and France, that wished to imbue the organization with supranational authority and others, fronted by the United Kingdom, Sweden, and Switzerland, who coveted intergovernmental arrangements. The latter's triumph left tensions festering between the functionalists and federalists that would contribute to the OEEC's eventual collapse. Irrespective in April 1948, the aforementioned 16 states (plus the United States and Canada as observers and later associate members) and the Commanders of the French, and joint British and American zones of Occupation in Germany (West Germany assumed membership in 1949) signed the OEEC Convention. Robert Marjolin, a distinguished French economist, became Secretary-General.

OEEC performance

Until recently, academic appraisals portrayed the OEEC as an institution in perennial crisis that played only a peripheral part in Western Europe's economic renaissance.[7] Contemporary scholarship is kinder, however, suggesting that the OEEC, before being overtaken by events, chalked up some noteworthy achievements, contributing to sharp rises in European trade, production, and investment and bequeathing a significant ideational and methodological legacy to global governance.[8]

The OEEC's intergovernmental makeup encumbered its ability to apportion Marshall Plan funds. The OEEC nonetheless produced annual recovery plans and administered the distribution of aid. To adjudicate between the competing claims of states, the OEEC introduced innovations whose impact on global governance would endure. The OEEC adopted embryonic versions of working routines such as peer review that would become the fulcrum of international economic surveillance at the OECD and elsewhere. To obtain funding, states had to submit economic programs detailing their requirements. The OEEC secretariat then prepared analyses of national programs before they were "exhaustively and critically examined, in the various committees of the organization, by representatives from all other member countries."[9] The absence of accurate and internationally comparable economic data hampered this process. To overcome this, the OEEC drew up a system of national accounts containing common definitions of key economic concepts, most famously Gross National Product (GNP), and standard statistical methodologies to measure them. The OEEC framework was later globalized owing to its almost wholesale incorporation into the UN's System of National Accounts.[10]

Researchers have also lavished praise on the OEEC's role in repairing Europe's faltering trade and payments system. Chronic balance of payments problems, a lack of currency convertibility, and a panoply of trade restrictions threatened initial ambitions to boost intra-European trade. The scarcity of US dollars, the one freely convertible currency, among European countries exacerbated these problems. Bilateral trade and payments agreements provided an interim solution but the desire of states to preserve their dollar reserves stalled trade growth. The negotiation within the OEEC of the European Payments Union (EPU) ultimately resolved this dilemma. Essentially, the EPU was a multilateral clearinghouse. Each month the EPU calculated the surpluses and deficits accumulated through bilateral trade and communicated this to the Bank for International Settlements (BIS). The BIS offset the various debts and surpluses every country had with its partners leaving them with a single debt or claim against the EPU. Surplus countries were remunerated by gold payments from, or extending credit to, the EPU. Deficit countries made payments in gold and received credit from the EPU. When the EPU's gold payments exceeded receipts, a fund of Marshall Plan dollars plugged the shortfall.[11] By obviating the need for swift bilateral payments in convertible currencies the EPU eased blockages to intra-OEEC trade. Easing payment difficulties hastened the OEEC's passage of The Code of Liberalization of Trade. Under the Code's auspices the percentage of private intra-OEEC trade subject to quantitative restrictions fell from 44 percent in 1950 to 6 percent in 1961[12] and the value of intra-European exports almost trebled to $2.2 billion. Flourishing intra-European trade lessened the continent's dependence on US imports permitting OEEC countries to accumulate dollar reserves and consolidate their financial position to the extent that all EPU members had reinstated currency convertibility by 1958.

The wording of the OEEC Convention implies it was always intended to outlive the Marshall Plan.[13] Nevertheless, the fizzling out of the Marshall Plan in 1951 prompted a bout of uncertainty that only ended when it was decided that the OEEC would become an economic adjunct to the North Atlantic Treaty Organization (NATO), the Western military alliance. This also spurred the OEEC's colonization of new tasks as the members sought to put European economic cooperation on a firmer footing. For example, the European Productivity Agency, a semi-autonomous agency housed at the OEEC from 1953, coordinated and provided technical assistance to national productivity agencies. In 1957, building upon the OEEC's existing work on energy, the OEEC became the home for the Nuclear Energy Agency charged with joint undertakings in the field of atomic power. Outside these operational activities, the OEEC's committees and working parties sowed the seeds of work that would germinate at the OECD. Founded in 1956, the Fiscal Committee's probing of double taxation provided the impetus for the 1963 OECD Model Tax Convention, today the cornerstone of a 3500 strong network of bilateral tax treaties.[14] Likewise, the Committee for Applied Research (1957) was the wellspring of OECD work on pollution and the Committee for Scientific and Technical Personnel paved the way for the economic implications of science and education to take their place on the OECD agenda.[15] The OEEC also dabbled in development issues with Europe's colonial powers coordinating their assistance to their dependencies through the Overseas Territories Committee.[16] The initiation of Working Party 19 of the Council (WP19) in 1956, the forerunner of the Economic Policy Committee (EPC), motioned moves toward tighter coordination of cyclical macroeconomic policies.[17] In summary, by the late 1950s, the OEEC was a venue where European countries were evolving a shared economic policy template through exchanging views, harmonizing outlooks and engineering norms to govern their growing interdependence.

Reincarnation: From OEEC to OECD (1958–61)

In 1955, Rene Sergent became Secretary-General. A senior French bureaucrat and Marjolin's erstwhile deputy, Sergent struggled to stamp his authority on an organization robbed of its earlier zest partly by virtue of its own success. By abetting the restoration of currency convertibility and whittling quantitative trade restrictions, the OEEC had helped rejuvenate the European economy and cured the headaches for which it was conceived. Together with the relative decline of US power and quarrels about European integration this elicited a reappraisal of transatlantic relationships that would lead to the OEEC's reincarnation as the OECD.

There were powerful arguments for conserving the machinery of transatlantic economic cooperation, not least preserving and managing the postwar economic interdependence fomented by the OEEC, but it was increasingly apparent that the organization was unbefitting for the task. First, Cold War enmities had intensified and the specter of communism loomed. Between 1953 and 1957, the USSR detonated its first hydrogen bomb, promulgated the Warsaw Pact (a military accord with its communist allies in Central and Eastern European), brutally suppressed uprisings in Poland and Hungary, and flaunted its possession of intercontinental ballistic missile technology by launching Sputnik, an earth orbiting satellite. Concurrently, US intervention in the Suez crisis had prejudiced its relationships with France and the UK, leaving NATO in disarray and redoubling the OEEC's value as a symbol of Western unity. Thanks to decolonization creating new suitors for the rival superpowers in the developing world, the Cold War battleground was also twisting from an East-West to a North-South axis. The Soviet "economic offensive"[18] in the developing world accentuated American concerns that if ideas and financial assistance were not forthcoming from the West these states would stray into the communist sphere. As a body appertaining to European development and designed to receive rather than generate development aid, the OEEC was poorly situated to discharge this role.

Second, by underwriting Europe's economic convalescence, the OEEC vitiated the constellation of power upon which it was premised. At the OEEC, the United States, as hegemon, had supplied aid and indulged trade discrimination to assist with rebuilding Europe's economies and solidify the Western alliance. Epitomized by its persistent trade deficit, an inevitable side-effect of European economic recuperation, was the attrition of the United States' relative power. The United States wanted the OEEC recalibrated to reflect this new distribution of power and to allocate more equitably the burden of bankrolling the liberal international economic order (LIEO).[19]

Third, the OEEC could no longer accommodate competing visions of European integration. In 1958, the latent schism between the OEEC's intergovernmentalists and its supranationalists erupted into open warfare when six members (Belgium, France, West Germany,

Italy, Luxembourg, and the Netherlands) established the European Economic Community (EEC), a common market with a common external tariff. Alarmed by the EEC's ambition for political union and the effects on their trade another seven states, led by the UK, pushed for an OEEC free trade area. This idea was halted by the United States, worried that this was a pretext to perpetuate discrimination against its exports, and France, which felt it would weaken EEC solidarity.[20] Intra-OEEC frictions culminated in the acrimonious dissolution of the OEEC Council's December 1958 meeting. Unable to conciliate between its members, the OEEC was rendered impotent.

Formal progress toward a fresh transatlantic organization began at a summit between the leaders of France, West Germany, the United Kingdom, and the United States in December 1959. Their communiqué called for a convocation of OEEC members to consider how consultations on trade, development, and regional integration should proceed. In January 1960, representatives of 13 countries, including the US and Canada, convened as the Special Economic Committee. This conclave established the Development Assistance Group (precursor to the OECD Development Assistance Committee (DAC)) and appointed "The Group of Four on Economic Organization" to confer with governments and make recommendations about the shape and functions of a new institution. After protracted and sometimes cantankerous consultations their testimony[21] called for a genuinely transatlantic body with the United States and Canada as full members and whose remit and nomenclature would hint at concerns with economic development worldwide. The Conference on the Reconstitution of the OEEC approved this formula in May 1960 and commissioned a working party to draft a founding charter. Two months later, a ministerial gathering endorsed the working party's labors and allotted a preparatory committee to finalize the charter and finesse the transition. On 14 December 1960, the OEEC members (numbering 18 since Spain's 1958 accession) plus Canada and the United States signed the OECD Convention.[22]

Relaunch: Thorkil Kristensen (1961–69)

In terms of its legal personality and working culture the OECD was virtually indistinguishable from its predecessor. Some notable exceptions aside, for example, the Code of Liberalization of Trade, most OEEC soft law and policy sectors were grandfathered into the OECD. Equally the OECD's additional members and more extensive empire necessitated some internal reshuffling.

The first OECD Secretary-General was Thorkil Kristensen. Appointed in July 1960 to oversee the transition from OEEC to OECD, he was well versed in the organization's ethos. An esteemed economist, Kristensen was intimately involved with the implementation of the Marshall Plan as Danish Minister of Finance (1945–47, 1950–53). As Danish representative in the Consultative Assembly of the Council of Europe (1949–58) and the Nordic Council (1953–60), he was likewise conversant with the internecine wrangling that sullied the OEEC's twilight years. Kristensen's incumbency was important because, following an historical institutionalist logic, his infant decisions had abiding repercussions for the organization. Under his leadership, the OECD most closely resembled the think tank with which it subsequently became synonymous. He wanted the OECD to be a fountain of groundbreaking ideas that could be peddled to its member clients. Kristensen conceived a primarily deliberative organization whose core work was "the continuing process of *consultation* in the widest sense."[23] Through this, bureaucrats in OECD countries would come to adhere to a common worldview and perception of economic problems and their solutions, providing a fertile ideational soil in which policy coordination could germinate. Cognizant of the need to fulfill the Convention and carve out a distinctive niche in global governance, the Secretary-General was also a cheerleader for stretching the OECD's appendages into "all aspects of economic life" including agriculture, industry, labor, education and science.[24]

The inaugural MCM in November 1961 proclaimed bold objectives for the organization's maiden decade, including a 50 percent expansion in the combined GNP of the OECD economies, attaining price stability and equilibrium in members' external payments, reducing trade barriers and fostering mutual approaches to development assistance. Improvized from superficial data and analyses, the growth target served multiple purposes. Symbolically the target was a signal of confidence in the Western economic model, its readiness to repel the Soviet threat, and address key societal tasks. Practically the target was about galvanizing Western economic cooperation, upholding commitments to promote sustainable economic expansion made in the Convention, and "affirming the OECD's ambitions in a new field of international policy-making."[25] Typifying its engagement with other sectors, the novelty of the policy area meant that much of the OECD's initial energies were expended erecting an intellectual scaffolding for understanding growth issues. As the 1960s wore on, OECD members came broadly to agree on a definition of, vocabulary to describe, statistical norms to compute, yardsticks to compare and policies to speed, economic growth. What the OECD was to contribute to the other tasks was initially unclear. The reinstatement of currency convertibility and proclivity for global rather than regional trade deals drew discussions of financial stability and trade into the ambit of the International Monetary Fund (IMF) and the General Agreement on Tariffs and Trade (GATT), respectively. Meanwhile the multilateral development banks appeared to have a stranglehold on international development. Events conspired, however, to ensure the OECD featured prominently in all three areas. In particular, frustration at slow progress in international organizations with universal memberships frequently led industrialized states to decant debates into the smaller, more homogenous OECD.

International financial management

The Bretton Woods fixed exchange rate system brought a modicum of order to international monetary relations. The system hinged on the United States' willingness to supply liquidity through a constant outflow of dollars and stability by guaranteeing to covert dollars into gold at a fixed rate. Inevitably the relentless pumping of dollars into the international financial system led to foreign dollar holdings exceeding US gold reserves, thereby undermining confidence in the United States' promise to exchange dollars at a fixed rate and exposing the currency to speculative attack.

Following a run on the dollar in 1960 the United States insisted on sturdier multilateral oversight to stabilize the international financial system. Logically this task fell within the IMF's purview but its swelling membership and European qualms about US dominance of the institution persuaded states to host these discussions at the OECD. Throughout the 1960s, the OECD, specifically its Working Party Number 3 on Policies for the Promotion of Better International Payments Equilibrium (WP3), was the hub for a phalanx of transgovernmental networks striving to superintend the strains beleaguering Bretton Woods.[26] A subgroup of the EPC, WP3 was hatched in 1961 at the behest of the US which desired an intimate setting where systemically important states could hold forthright and confidential exchanges about the international financial system. WP3 consisted of high-ranking officials from the central banks and finance ministries of Canada, France, Germany, Italy, Japan (after 1964), the Netherlands, Sweden, Switzerland, the United Kingdom, the United States, and delegates from the European Commission, IMF and BIS. The novelty of the bi-monthly WP3 meeting, and hence their strict secrecy, was that participants were expected to relinquish classified information to their counterparts about the policies they were contemplating. At an abstract level, WP3 debates were about state-market relationships in international financial governance. More concretely, the WP3 sought to coordinate policies to correct balance of payments disequilibria and, anticipating the neoliberal onslaught, sponsor capital account liberalization.

The secrecy surrounding WP3 impairs assessments of its impact. Indubitably WP3 sessions moderated frictions by cultivating camaraderie among national officials and inculcating them with the ability to predict the actions and likely reactions of their counterparts to chosen strategies.[27] WP3 also animated the search for better data and models to forecast balance of payments trends. Yet many remain skeptical. Even when officials reached a robust consensus in WP3, this seldom educed decisive shifts in their own central bank or finance ministry, let alone the wider circles of national economic policymaking.[28]

International trade

Despite being conspicuous in the Convention, the OECD appeared destined for a tangential role in the global trading regime. The wounds from the skirmishes between the EEC "six" and what in 1960 became the European Free Trade Association (EFTA) "seven" were yet to heal. The North American countries meanwhile, suspicious of its potential as a tool of European protectionism, had opposed carrying the Code of Liberalization forward to the OECD. They preferred a global approach to trade liberalization, championing the GATT as the spearhead for this enterprise.[29] GATT's limitations, however, meant that its propensity for trade liberalization was often contingent on prior or parallel activity in the OECD.

Under GATT, states had successfully negotiated rules to prune tariffs on industrial and manufactured goods but more stubborn issues now intruded. Partly this stemmed from the difficulty of corralling consensus among GATT's increasingly diverse membership. Whereas 26 states including seven developing countries participated in the 1960–61 Dillon Round trade negotiations, 62 states including 25 developing nations joined the 1964–67 Kennedy Round. GATT's tiny Secretariat curbed its capacity to undertake the detailed technical and analytical studies required to supply states with the consensual knowledge needed to identify and frame their interests. As frustration with the gridlocked GATT mounted, the OECD Trade Committee with its supporting secretariat, likeminded membership and less legalistic approach, surfaced as a prenegotiating forum. The Trade Committee fathomed and sought rules to govern trade issues of disproportionate interest to OECD countries and to prepare them for insertion in future GATT rounds.

The case of government procurement exemplifies the Trade Committee's role. A crucial component of national economic and security policy, government procurement was omitted from GATT's national treatment and most-favored nation principles. The tendency of governments to indulge domestic bidders when awarding contracts made procurement rules a noteworthy trade impediment. The Trade Committee's major work started in 1964 with a review of member procurement practices. The ensuing report was the first wide-ranging comparative analysis of government procurement rules and revealed the extent of the bias toward indigenous suppliers. In 1967, the Secretariat presented a draft text on government procurement guidelines which were followed by proposals by the US and European Community (EC). An amalgam of these recommendations yielded a draft OECD code on government procurement liberalization. The code was non-binding but the substance, including the principle that rules should not prejudice against overseas tenders, became the crux of government procurement negotiations in the 1973–79 Tokyo Round.

International development

By 1970, the norm that advanced states should pledge development assistance to their less fortunate counterparts was widely accepted. Similarly, the field of international development cooperation was structured around agreed definitions of what constitutes development aid, principles about how much aid governments should provide, to whom and on what terms, mathematical methods to compute, compare and evaluate aid giving, and surveillance to assess whether states were honoring their aid obligations. None of this existed in 1960 and its emergence owed a substantial debt to the DAC.

DAC's members rejected the possibility of it pursuing an operational mandate, and it instead became the crucible in which they forged the international development cooperation paradigm. In March 1961, the members of what was then still the DAG endorsed the Resolution of the Common Aid Effort committing members to expand the volume, soften the terms, and enhance the effectiveness of financial assistance to developing countries.[30] To ensure aid effectiveness, and to respond to US overtures for European countries share more of the burden, the DAC needed to concoct a uniform definition of development aid.

Hynes and Scott have dissected the tortuous process through which the DAC came to settle on a definition of Official Development Assistance (ODA) that confines it to those financial flows which possess a primarily developmental motivation, official character and are awarded on concessional terms.[31] This yardstick gained global acclaim in 1970 when the UN adopted a target for donors to provide ODA equivalent to 0.7 percent of their GNI. The DAC contrived statistical conventions to appraise and juxtapose national development efforts with "the whole statistical picture of international development finance……largely the product of the OECD Secretariat."[32] Alongside quantifying development assistance, the DAC distilled the experiences and perspectives of members into a suite of best practice guidelines. The DAC also helped constitute new actors in the development field. Whereas development was once a fringe activity with rudimentary administrative structures strewn across many government ministries, the consistency demanded by DAC's peer reviews coaxed many states to create dedicated development departments. In short, within a decade the DAC had molded a loose coalition of countries making vague pledges of benevolence toward the less fortunate into "a community of aid donors, sharing a more or less coherent doctrine on aid questions."[33]

For all this, after peaking at 0.54 percent of GDP in 1961, the proportion of ODA from DAC members drifted downward. Resentment about the paternalism of international development cooperation, the scarcity of aid, and inequities in the global trade regime led to OECD countries being ambushed by developing countries at the first United Nations Conference on Trade and Development (UNCTAD) in 1964. The UNCTAD ordeal exposed divisions within the OECD, especially on trade. Afterward the DAC's Working Party on UNCTAD issues became a place where DAC members could iron out their differences prior to future UN meetings.[34]

Renown: Emile van Lennep (1969–84)

Emile van Lennep became Secretary-General in October 1969 after 18 years as Treasurer General of the Netherlands Ministry of Finance. Deeply immersed in global financial governance, van Lennep previously held illustrious OECD portfolios including chair of WP3 and vice chair of the EPC. An entrepreneurial Secretary-General, van Lennep stressed the importance of the OECD producing ideas and analyses that were relevant to member states. Under his leadership the OECD grew geographically, with the accessions of Australia and New Zealand,[35] and functionally, deftly manipulating the economic paroxysms unleashed by the collapse of Bretton Woods (1971) and the oil crisis (1973) to justify its infiltration of new provinces including the environment, corporate governance, financial and fiscal affairs. The unrelenting economic turbulence kindled debates around the prescriptions for economic growth and the efficacy of the arrangements for global economic governance. A harbinger of the neoliberal revolution, the OECD's work was reoriented toward eliminating impediments to efficient market operations. Industrialized countries used the OECD to organize their resistance against calls for a New International Economic Order (NIEO), a package to overhaul the rules and institutions of global economic governance in favor of the developing nations.[36] Nonetheless, by trespassing on its core competencies, other multilateral economic institutions were diminishing OECD prerogatives.

The growth conundrum

Even before the tumultuous events of the 1970s, a lively debate was under way in the OECD Secretariat about the nature and meaning of economic growth. The target set in 1961 was exceeded but now, under the umbrella of a project entitled "the problems of modern society," a faction of OECD bureaucrats rotating around the organization's science division, critiqued the emphasis on quantitative economic growth. Their denunciation centered on the unwanted social and environmental effects of economic growth. Ignored in national income accounts, these externalities are antithetical to the injunction in Article 1 of the OECD Convention to foster rising living standards. This critique fell from grace in tandem with plummeting growth rates whereupon the orthodox economists of the Economics and Statistics Department, whose concentration on output aligned with the interests of powerful OECD members, reasserted their ascendency.[37] Regardless, this debate had lasting consequences for the organization.

Alongside the economic crisis and the emergence of stagflation, the economic growth debate prompted murmurings about the economic philosophy underpinning the OECD's pursuit of its foremost mission. Once a crusader for the Keynesian creed the OECD mutated slowly but palpably into a proselytizer of the neoliberal gospel. OECD reports censuring precepts of the Keynesian consensus and espousing supply side dogmas had been syndicated since 1970 but only at the end of the decade did the latter start to supplant the former in country reports, ministerial communiqués and landmark studies such as the McCracken Report. The puzzle of lethargic economic growth was reimagined as one of excessive government intervention and structural impediments to market operations. Henceforth, the routes to stellar economic performance were "positive adjustment policies": flexible labor markets, deregulation, reduced protectionism and cutting welfare expenditure. Whether the OECD was the "ideational artist" in the vanguard of this intellectual revolution or an "ideational agent" condoning existing trends to ingratiate it with national capitals and other international organizations is a vexed question.[38] Most diagnoses conclude that powerful state interests drove the OECD's conversion rather than vice versa.[39]

Disputes over economic growth sealed the environment's place on the OECD's agenda. Work on the environment, principally pollution, was carried over from the OEEC but was scattered across various directorates and was technically rather than politically oriented. Many international organizations were eyeing the environment as a subject that could cement their relevance to their members. The OECD's combination of existing technical expertise, exclusion of the developing states, and economic construction of environmental issues ultimately secured it the job. OECD states wanted environmental issues presented in a manner ostensibly compatible with free-market capitalism.[40] Prior negotiation at the OECD would make it easier for members to ensure this vision of environmental governance triumphed globally.

In 1970, the OECD became the first international organization to establish a permanent directorate devoted to the environment. At this stage, none of the members had an environment ministry and this scarcity of national knowhow meant the OECD exerted considerable influence over this formative domain.[41] The OECD became a renowned source of authoritative environmental data and assisted members to establish policies that would assuage environmental problems without retarding economic growth. Indeed, the OECD's environmental agenda was piloted overwhelmingly by economic concerns. Economists rather than ecologists oversaw the work, and their primary focus was not reducing environmental destruction but stopping states disguising trade protection as environmental rules. Through the Environment Committee, the OECD elaborated soft law covering inter alia: movement of hazardous waste, water pollution, use and management, recycling, transboundary pollution, prevention and control of oil spills, and limiting energy use. Many of the concepts contained in these conventions would appear subsequently in global environmental agreements, most strikingly the "polluter pays principle" from the 1972 Guiding Principles Concerning the International Economic Aspects of Environmental Policies.[42]

Responding to the oil crisis

In autumn 1973, the Organization of the Petroleum Exporting Countries (OPEC) engineered a quadrupling of oil prices by embargoing supplies. This sparked a frantic search among OECD countries for funds to pay escalating import bills and mitigate their vulnerability to future shocks. Sensing an opportunity to rectify rifts in the Western alliance caused by commercial strains and the Vietnam War, the United States propounded a countervailing consortium of oil consumers. As a body containing the Western powers, the world's prominent purchasers, and with extant oil and energy committees, the OECD was a logical site for this. In November 1974, 16 countries adopted a Council Decision establishing the International Energy Agency (IEA). Lodged at the OECD and serviced by the Secretariat, the IEA was an autonomous body with a separate governing board. This peculiar configuration arose because not all OECD members belonged to the IEA. Indeed, the IEA negotiation was not straightforward. Opposition rested on apprehension that the IEA was a contraption of US hegemony whose confrontational stance could jeopardize access to OPEC supplies. To sweeten the deal, the US proposed a Financial Support Fund, a $25 billion loan and guarantee facility, to be managed by and for the benefit of OECD members. This incited an institutional tussle with the IMF, which felt the Financial Support Fund threatened its role as international lender of last resort. Despite intense OECD lobbying a chain of events, culminating in a failure to gain legislative ratification in the US, conspired to see the Financial Support Fund was stillborn, dealing a blow to the OECD's quest to consolidate its place in global economic governance.[43]

The IEA's main features were an emergency oil sharing scheme, augmented data about energy markets and the instigation of a long-term plan to trim oil dependency. The fallout from the oil crisis was less severe than had been initially feared with most countries locating finance to cope with higher prices. Notwithstanding the oil price hike of 1979, OPEC's threat also began to dissipate. IEA contingency plans have been invoked in response to actual and threatened disruptions, and it continues to inspect national policies and to organize emergency response exercises to maintain preparedness. Nonetheless, cooperation at the IEA predominantly became about monitoring and developing concepts, statistics and models to comprehend the complexities of the international energy system. The IEA's authoritative data and analysis would go on to inform the deliberations of a host of international initiatives at the G7, G20, and the United Nations

Framework Convention on Climate Change (UNFCCC) among others (see Chapter 5).

Trade

Deteriorating economic conditions heightened protectionist pressures. The OECD checked this by chivvying along the Tokyo Round, sculpting the agenda for, and dowsing discord in, the Uruguay Round (1986-94), and clinching informal compacts on trade topics unready for GATT negotiations. Following the Tokyo Round, tentative steps toward fresh negotiations were taken in the OECD. Exhorted by the 1981 MCM to trigger a program to scan the trade horizon, the OECD produced *Trade Issues in the 1980s*. This was the bedrock of the Trade Committee's input to agricultural and services trade without which the realization of the Uruguay Round would have been "inconceivable."[44]

Until the 1970s, states did not deem services as rightful ingredients of the GATT regime. Service transactions were thought distinct from merchandise trade because they could not be transported or stored and vendors often had to travel with their product. Before services could be subject to GATT disciplines the idea first had to be established that services were tradable.[45] The notion of "trade in services" was first mooted in 1972 by the OECD High Level Group on Trade and Related Problems. The OECD fleshed out the concept and transformed the attitudes of members and, a decade later, the bulk of them were reconciled to services being legitimate targets of GATT ordinances. Nevertheless, services were not yet ripe for negotiation. Many OECD countries were dubious about the merits of liberalizing trade in services and, reminiscent of government procurement, states lacked "a theoretical foundation on which to construct a set of rules."[46] The OECD dissolved these obstacles by furnishing states with evidence about the importance of services to their economic well-being and a "conceptual framework for service trade modeled on fundamental GATT principles"[47] and the subject booked its place on the Uruguay Round agenda.

Agricultural trade was incorporated in GATT but exemptions authorizing the use of quantitative restrictions and subsidies plus squabbles among major producers precluded negotiations. The OECD had extensively investigated domestic agricultural questions but only with the formation of a joint working party of the Trade and Agriculture Committees in 1979 was there any serious interrogation of agricultural *trade*. Their 1982 report *Problems of Agriculture* demonstrated the wastefulness of government intervention, its distorting effects on agricultural trade, and validated the idea that agriculture should go forward to the GATT. Under the rubric of the Ministerial Trade Mandate, the OECD equipped the negotiators with the conceptual and empirical knowledge needed to consummate the talks. The OECD invented aggregate measurements of agricultural subsidies that allowed states to accurately compare the costs of protectionism and pinpoint the impact of liberalization.[48]

The OECD also continued to provide a framework where states agreed soft law instruments for topics proving intractable elsewhere or of disproportionate interest to the members. Its most arresting achievement was in the field of export credits, preferential borrowing terms offered by developed countries to encourage developing countries to purchase their products. The Trade Committee had studied export credits since 1963 after the divergent interests of developed and developing states stalled headway in the Berne Union. The onset of tougher economic conditions raised the prospect of a race to the bottom with OECD countries gifting ever more generous terms to bolster their domestic producers. The OECD was the forum of choice because it included all major purveyors of export credits but excluded net recipients likely to oppose to rules to limit it. Building on studies by the OECD's Group on Export Credit and Export Credit Guarantees, and assisted by the G7, 20 states approved the Arrangement on Guidelines for Officially Supported Export Credits in 1978 stipulating the most charitable credit terms signatories may offer. Over the next decade, revisions to the Arrangement made it more stringent and applicable to more industries helping to nullify the competitive element of export credits for capital goods.[49]

Institutional competition

The 1970s economic emergencies inflamed the debate about the architecture of global economic governance and the OECD's place within it. Other institutions were encroaching onto the OECD's strongholds. In development, the World Bank was providing "much of the necessary research, coordination, setting of standards, goals etc., that came mainly from the OECD a decade ago."[50] Reform to the IMF's Articles of Agreement boosted its surveillance functions at the OECD's expense.[51] The OECD's grip on macroeconomic policy coordination loosened when leading members started making commitments in the G7 family. The OECD Secretariat's exclusion from the G7 Summit preparations likewise diminished the organization's power (see Chapter 2).[52] A posse of G7 ministerial groupings including the Quadrilateral Group of Trade Ministers and the Finance Ministers and Central Bank Governors impinged directly on the OECD's customary ground. For example, the finance ministers masterminded international efforts to manage balance of payments problems including the Plaza Accord (1985) and, with fewer senior figures attending, the WP3 was relegated to the sidelines.[53] Finally, the OECD faced competition from revitalized European integration. The signing of the Single European Act in 1986 promised the EC's members, whose numbers had doubled since 1973, a single market and stronger EC bodies. Comprising half of the OECD membership and proficient across a breadth of issues, the EC was an attractive venue for their cooperative ventures.

Conclusion

When van Lennep exited in 1984, he left an organization entrenched as an authoritative actor across a multitude of international regimes. The OECD was renowned for the reliability of its data, the integrity of its analysis, and its capacity to elucidate rules for knotty or emergent problems. These rules often became de facto global standards courtesy of the OECD members accounting for four-fifths of economic output and operating as a caucus in international organizations with all-encompassing memberships. Bearing the hallmarks of US hegemony, the OECD was an avowedly Western body where the countries of the free world soothed their economic interdependence and orchestrated their resistance to proposals from the Global South for radical changes to multilateral rules and institutions. The OECD had normalized economic growth as the primary economic goal but anemic growth rates in the post-Bretton Woods era and the accompanying economic upheavals sapped the organization's legitimacy. Besieged by institutional competitors, the OECD was about to enter a period of retrenchment.

Notes

1 Quoted in "Bretton Woods Decisions," *Pillars of Peace: Documents pertaining to American interest in establishing a lasting world peace, January 1941-February 1946* (Carlisle, P.A.: Book Department Army Information School), 32.
2 G. John Ikenberry, *Liberal Leviathan: The Origins, Crisis, and Transformation of the American World Order* (Princeton, N.J.: Princeton University Press, 2011), chapter 5.

3 Matthieu Leimgruber and Matthias Schmelzer, eds., *The OECD and the International Political Economy Since 1948* (Basingstoke: Palgrave, 2017), Part I.
4 Matthias Schmelzer, *The Hegemony of Growth: The OECD and the Making of the Economic Growth Paradigm* (Cambridge: Cambridge University Press, 2016).
5 John G. Ruggie, "International Regimes, Transactions, and Change: Embedded Liberalism in the Postwar Economic Order," *International Organization* 36, no. 2 (1982): 379–415.
6 "Mr X" [George F. Kennan], "The Sources of Soviet Conduct," *Foreign Affairs* 25, no. 4 (1948): 420–26.
7 See for example Alan S. Milward, *The Reconstruction of Western Europe, 1945–51* (London: Methuen, 1984), 168–211.
8 Matthieu Leimgruber and Matthias Schmelzer, "From the Marshall Plan to Global Governance: Historical Transformations of the OEEC/OECD, 1948 to Present," in *The OECD and the International Political Economy Since 1948*, eds. Matthieu Leimgruber and Matthias Schmelzer (Basingstoke: Palgrave, 2017), 28–33. Schmelzer, *The Hegemony of Growth*, 38–45.
9 OECD Observer, "Twenty Nations Exchange Their Policy Ideas for Mutual Economic Benefit," *OECD Observer* no. 3 (1963): 4.
10 Schmelzer, *The Hegemony of Growth*, chapter 1; Andre Vanoli, *A History of National Accounting* (Amsterdam: IOS Press, 2005), 132.
11 On the origins and working of the EPU see Kurt F. Flexner, "The Creation of the European Payments Union: An Example in International Compromise," *Political Science Quarterly* 72, no. 2 (1957): 241–60; James J. Kaplan and Gunther Schleiminger, *The European Payments Union: Financial Diplomacy in the 1950s* (Oxford: Clarendon Press, 1989).
12 OEEC, *O.E.E.C. 12th Annual Economic Review*, C(61)116 Annex, 11 July 1961, 71.
13 Henry J.B. Lintott, "The Organization for European Economic Cooperation," *International Organization* 3, no. 2 (1949): 269.
14 Sol Picciotto, *International Business Taxation: A Study in the Internationalization of Business Regulation* (London: Weidenfield and Nicholson, 1992), 52–54.
15 Regula Burgi, "Engineering the Free World: The Emergence of the OECD as an Actor in Education Policy, 1957–1972," in *The OECD and the International Political Economy Since 1948*, eds. Matthieu Leimgruber and Matthias Schmelzer (Basingstoke: Palgrave, 2017), 287.
16 Matthias Schmelzer, "A Club of the Rich to Help the Poor? The OECD, "Development", and the Hegemony of Donor Countries," in *International Organizations and Development, 1945–1990*, eds. Marc Frey, Sonke Kunkel and Corinna R. Unger (Basingstoke: Palgrave, 2014), 171–95; Schmelzer, *The Hegemony of Growth*, 217–23.
17 Schmelzer, ibid., 160–61.
18 Willard L. Thorp, "American Policy and the Soviet Economic Offensive," *Foreign Affairs* 35, no. 2 (1957): 271–82.
19 William Diebold Jr., "Economic Aspects of an Atlantic Community," *International Organization* 17, no. 3 (1963): 671–73.

20 See Emile Benoit, *Europe at Sixes and Sevens: The Common Market, the Free Trade Association and the United States* (New York: Columbia University Press, 1961); Richard T. Griffiths, ""An Act of Creative Leadership": The end of the OEEC and the Birth of the OECD," in *Explorations in OEEC History*, ed. Richard T. Griffiths (Paris: OECD, 1997), 236–42.
21 OEEC, *A Remodeled Economic Organisation: A Report by the Group of Four* (Paris: OEEC, 1960).
22 This process is outlined in greater detail by Hugo J. Hahn, "Continuity in the Law of International Organization. Part Two: Continuity from OEEC to OECD," *Duke Law Journal* 11, no. 4 (1962): 532–34; Schmelzer, *The Hegemony of Growth*, 45–53.
23 Thorkil Kristensen, "Five Years of O.E.C.D.," in *European Yearbook Volume XIII*, ed. The Council of Europe (The Hague: Martinus Nijhoff, 1967), 105 (emphasis in original).
24 See for example OECD, *The Work and Programme of the Organisation: Report by the Secretary-General to the Ministerial Council of the O.E.C.D. 27th-28th November 1962*, C(62)180, 10 November 1962, 5.
25 Schmelzer, *The Hegemony of Growth*, 185.
26 Kazuhiko Yago, "A Crisis Manager for the International Monetary and Financial System? The Rise and Fall of the OECD Working Party 3, 1961-1980," in *The OECD and the International Political Economy Since 1948*, eds. Matthieu Leimgruber and Matthias Schmelzer (Basingstoke: Palgrave, 2017), 187–92.
27 Robert W. Russell, "Transgovernmental Interaction in the International Monetary System, 1960–1972," *International Organization* 27, no. 4 (1973): 457–58.
28 John S. Odell, *U.S. International Monetary Policy: Markets, Power and Ideas as Sources of Change* (Princeton, N.J.: Princeton University Press, 1982), 349–50.
29 Theodore H. Cohn, *Governing Global Trade: International Institutions in Conflict and Convergence* (Aldershot: Ashgate, 2002), 43.
30 OECD, *Resolution of the United States Delegation on the Common Aid Effort*, DAG4 Doc23 (Second Revision) 29 March 1961.
31 William M. Hynes and Simon Scott, "The Evolution of Official Development Assistance: Achievements, Criticisms and a Way Forward," *OECD Development Co-operation Working Papers* No.12.
32 Goran Ohlin, "The Organization for Economic Cooperation and Development," *International Organization* 22, no. 1 (1968): 238.
33 Schmelzer, "A Club of the Rich to Help the Poor?," 172.
34 Patricia Hongler, "The Construction of a Western Voice: OECD and the First UNCTAD of 1964," in *The OECD and the International Political Economy Since 1948*, eds. Matthieu Leimgruber and Matthias Schmelzer (Basingstoke: Palgrave, 2017), 137–61.
35 Peter Carroll, "Shall We or Shall We Not? The Japanese, Australian, and New Zealand Decisions to Apply for Membership in the OECD, 1960–1973," in *The OECD and the International Political Economy Since 1948*, eds. Matthieu Leimgruber and Matthias Schmelzer (Basingstoke: Palgrave, 2017), 113–37.
36 Jeffrey A. Hart, *The New International Economic Order: Conflict and Cooperation in North-South Economic Relations, 1974–77* (Basingstoke: Palgrave, 1983), chapter 5.

37 Schmelzer, *The Hegemony of Growth*, chapter 7 and 8.
38 Martin Marcussen, "The OECD in Search of a Role: Playing the Idea Game," Paper presented at the European Consortium for Political Research, Grenoble, 6–11 April 2001, 1.
39 Samuel Beroud, ""Positive Adjustments": The Emergence of Supply-Side Economics in the OECD and G7, 1970–1984," in *The OECD and the International Political Economy Since 1948*, eds. Matthieu Leimgruber and Matthias Schmelzer (Basingstoke: Palgrave, 2017), 233–58; Vincent Gayon, *The McCracken Report or the OECD Response to the "Crisis": Writing and Prescribing in Uncertain Times* (Paris: OECD, 2015).
40 Matthias Schmelzer, "'Born in the Corridors of the OECD': The Forgotten Origins of the Club of Rome, Transnational Networks, and the 1970s in Global History," *Journal of Global History* 12, no. 2 (2012): 46.
41 Iris Bowery, "(Re-)Thinking Environment and Economy: The OECD and Sustainable Development," in *International Organizations and Environmental Policies*, eds. Wolfram Kaiser and Jan-Henrik Meyer (New York: Berghahn Books, 2016), 211–40.
42 Jonathan Nash, "Too Much Market? Conflict Between Tradable Pollution Allowances and the Polluter Pays Principle," *Harvard Environmental Law Review* 24, no. 2 (2000): 465–535.
43 Benjamin J. Cohen, "The Financial Support Fund of the OECD: A Failed Initiative," *Princeton University International Finance Section Essays in International Finance* 204 (1997).
44 Robert Wolfe, *The Making of the Peace, 1993: The OECD in Canadian Economic Diplomacy* (Kingston, Canada: Queen's University, 1993), 43.
45 William J. Drake and Kalypso Nicolaidis, "Ideas, Interests and Institutions: 'Trade in Services' and the Uruguay Round," *International Organization* 46, no. 1 (1992): 41–53.
46 Ronald K. Shelp, "Trade in Services," *Foreign Policy* no. 64 (1986): 64.
47 Ibid., 72.
48 Cohn, *Governing Global Trade*, 147–53, 182–84.
49 Andrew M. Moravcsik, "Disciplining trade finance: the OECD Export Credit Arrangement," *International Organization* 46, no. 1 (1989): 184–86.
50 Miriam Camps, *"First World" Relationships: The Role of the OECD* (Paris: The Atlantic Institute for International Affairs, 1975), 29.
51 Louis W. Pauly, "The Political Foundations of Multilateral Economic Surveillance," *International Journal* 47, no. 2 (1992): 293–327.
52 Emile van Lennep, "Institutional aspects of international economic policy cooperation and coordination," in *The Reality of International Economic Policy Coordination*, ed. Hendrikus J. Blommerstein (Amsterdam, Holland: Elsevier Science Publishers, 1998), 279–80.
53 Yoichi Funabashi, *Managing the Dollar: From the Plaza to the Louvre* (Washington, D.C.: Institute for International Economics, 1988); Kazuhiko Yago, "A Crisis Manager for the International Monetary and Financial System?," 201.

2 The OECD, 1984-present

From retrenchment to redemption?

This chapter narrates the OECD story from 1984 until 2021, outlining and analyzing the organization's bearing on, and place in, the architecture of global governance during the tenures of three Secretary-Generals: Jean-Claude Paye, Donald Johnston, and Angel Gurria. During this time, the OECD, and the geopolitical context and ideational content of its operations, underwent drastic changes that would see the institution's future called into doubt.

Within six years of Claude-Paye's appointment, the Berlin Wall, whose construction commenced a month before the ratification of the OECD Convention, was breached signifying the beginning of the end of the Cold War. Embodying the capitalist and democratic values of the triumphant West, the OECD appeared destined for a golden age amidst US President George W. Bush's recently proclaimed new world order. Unfortunately, this post-Cold War euphoria would prove fleeting with the discrediting of its most plausible ideological adversary plunging the OECD into an identity crisis. Even if it was simplistic to regard the OECD purely as a Cold War warrior, the melting of the Iron Curtain intensified questions about the organization's personality and its place in the global governance architecture. The struggle to articulate answers around which members can coalesce has bedeviled the OECD ever since (see also Chapter 6). These woes were exacerbated by wider realignments in the global balance of power. In contrast to the Cold War era, when global power redistributions occurred principally *among* OECD members, since 1990 the main feature has been the redistribution of power *between* OECD and non-OECD countries. Collectively, the OECD still looms large in the global economy but, as Table 2.1 highlights, its ascendance is receding. As its dominance dwindled, voices criticizing the logic or legitimacy of using the OECD as a forum for the discussion and development of global rules grew louder.

DOI: 10.4324/9781351025867-3

Table 2.1 Key global trends—OECD percentage shares

	1960	*1970*	*1980*	*1990*	*2000*	*2010*	*2020*
Population	16.4	19.3	17.9	16.2	18.5	17.6	17.3
GNI (current US$)	77.5	80.6	79.2	83.2	82.2	68.6	61.6 (2019)
GNI (PPP, current international US$)	-	-	-	62.5	60.3	49.7	46.7
Merchandise trade exports	52.8	65.0	58.6	67.6	70.3	59.4	58.2
Merchandise trade imports	51.4	65.6	74.4	69.1	74.3	63.2	61.3
CO2 emissions	54.9	58.4	51.3	48.2	54.3	40.1	35.3
Outward FDI Flow	-	97.3	93.5	88.4	88.8	70.7	72.0
Inward FDI Flow	-	63.6	86.2	82.9	83.8	51.9	54.7
Outward FDI Stock	-	-	87.4	93.1	90.7	83.6	77.2
Inward FDI Stock	-	-	59.0	77.0	80.2	67.5	68.4

Sources: Derived from UN, *World Population Prospects 2019*, https://population.un.org/wpp/; World Bank, *World Development Indicators Database*, https://databank.worldbank.org/source/world-development-indicators; World Trade Organization Data Portal, https://data.wto.org/; Our World in Data, "CO2 and Greenhouse Gas Emissions," https://ourworldindata.org/co2-and-other-greenhouse-gas-emissions#production-vs-consumption-based-emissions-over-time; UNCTADStat, https://unctadstat.unctad.org/EN/

Ideational tremors accompanied those in the geopolitical landscape. Promoting policies to achieve economic growth persisted as a core OECD objective but the ideas informing its prescriptions evolved. The last remnants of Keynesianism were purged and, although they were arguably more eclectic than those of the international financial institutions, the OECD's outputs acquired a distinctly neoliberal tinge. Accordingly, the OECD now maintained that the route to stable, non-inflationary growth lay in unleashing the power of market competition and individual enterprise through liberalization, deregulation, and privatization. This version of capitalism, and its conceptualization of the correct relationship between states and markets, differed fundamentally from the Keynesian embedded liberal compromise that dominated the formative phase of OECD history (see Chapter 1). Whereas Keynesianism extolled state intervention to buffer economies and societies against the full effects of market forces, neoliberalism prescribed their exposure to market disciplines to incentivize individual risk taking and entrepreneurship. The turn to "turbocapitalism,"[1] however, would strain the union between the two creeds central to the OECD's identity: capitalism and democracy. Neoliberal capitalism bred inequity, insecurity, and instability, the latter exemplified by the

Global Financial Crisis of 2008 and the former by the austerity policies that followed it, inducing widespread alienation with democratic institutions and processes. The ensuing decade of anemic growth and political paroxysm across the OECD laid bare the difficulties of reconciling the inegalitarian outcomes of capitalism with the egalitarian customs of democracy.[2] This dulled the luster of the OECD model of democratic capitalism, not just as something to which others should aspire but also amongst the organization's members.

Coping with these geopolitical and ideational developments occasioned modifications in the OECD's character and remit. First, the inward-oriented OECD of the Cold War era was gradually superseded by an outward looking organization with global pretensions. Since 1994, the OECD community has almost doubled in size (see Table I.1), transforming the organization from a predominantly 'Western' club to one boasting members from all bar the African continent. With economic globalization coupling the member's fortunes to the rest of the global economy, the OECD went from an organization that talked *about* non-members to one that talked *to* them.[3] Non-member states were invited to participate in an array of OECD committees and projects (see also Chapters 3 and 6), which were also made more amenable to inputs from international organizations and civil society organizations (CSOs).

Second, the adoption of the neoliberal mantra further tweaked the genre of cooperation at the OECD away from *international* policy coordination toward pinpointing, and pressuring states to implement, an appropriate retinue of *domestic* policies. Reflecting faith in the self-equilibrating nature of markets, the OECD felt that if states put their domestic houses in order this would lessen the need for formal international coordination. Finally, the recourse to neoliberalism also turned up the heat on debates that had simmered at the OECD since the 1960s about the nature and sources of economic growth (see Chapter 1) and the suitability of GDP growth as a policy objective or bellwether of human progress. Rising GDP remained paramount, but the OECD placed greater emphasis on economic policies to promote environmental sustainability, social inclusion, and life satisfaction.[4] This "humanisation of material progress," pithily expressed since 2011 in the OECD's strapline "better policies for better lives," together with the search for suitable domestic policy templates rejuvenated the organization's work in health, education, labor markets, and taxation.

The remainder of the chapter is structured as follows. The next section analyses the OECD's retrenchment under Jean Claude Paye (1984–96). During his stint, the OECD made many important contributions to global governance, for example, to the G7 system and nascent discussions of climate change. The redrawing of the international system at the end of the Cold War, however, threatened to consign to irrelevance an organization already squeezed by institutional competition. This sets the context for the third section, which examines Donald Johnston's (1996–2006) attempts to reinvent the organization by "getting to grips with globalisation."[5] The sudden salience of tax transparency and education governance, issues where the OECD had substantial expertise, compensated for the attenuation of traditional OECD functions such as trade. Internal reorganization, an expansion of the organization's field of vision, and a wave of enlargement and enhanced engagement with non-members arrested the OECD's decline and lay the foundation, considered in section four, for Angel Gurria's (2006–21) shot at redemption. Bookended by the global financial crisis and the coronavirus, in-between Gurria made great strides toward his stated aim of remaking the OECD as a "hub of globalisation."[6] Through a relentless focus on relevance to members and a methodical approach to engaging non-members, especially those in the G20, the OECD enhanced its profile and today sits at the interstices of transgovernmental networks governing cutting edge issues from artificial intelligence (AI) and sustainable investment to crypto currency and climate change. These achievements are nonetheless vulnerable to contradictions in the OECD's outreach strategy (see Chapter 6) and the vicissitudes of global politics (see Chapter 7). The fifth section reflects on the OEEC and OECD's contribution to global governance and briefly introduces Mathias Cormann, who assumed office in June 2021.

Retrenchment: Jean-Claude Paye (1984–96)

Jean-Claude Paye, a French bureaucrat and diplomat, became OECD Secretary-General in October 1984. Postings in the European Commission and the French civil service, including as a "sherpa" to the G7, gave Paye a good grasp of OECD politics. Echoing his predecessors, Paye envisaged the OECD as an "analyst and catalyst"[7] collecting, analyzing, and disseminating data, ideas and evidence as a basis for enlightened policymaking and international cooperation. The fundamental continuity of the organization's role contrasted with drastic upheavals in the philosophical and geopolitical backdrop of its operations. The sluggish record of OECD economies in the decade leading up to Paye's appointment had strengthened the hand of those arguing that the solution lay in unleashing the power of market forces.

Having dissected them for a quarter of a century or more, the OECD had a comparative advantage in subjects like labor markets, competition policy, education, and public sector governance that were suddenly in vogue. Regrettably, the reputational recompense to the OECD from the lionization of "structural" policy reform was outweighed by the damage inflicted by changes in its external environment. The disintegration of authoritarianism and central planning in the former communist block was a victory for OECD convictions about the superiority of capitalism and democracy as organizing principles for global governance. Suddenly bereft of its communist nemesis, however, the OECD, a quintessentially Western organization (see Chapter 1), looked anachronistic. What, in a post-Cold War world, was the OECD for? Ultimately, Paye's inability to orchestrate a compelling answer to this question sealed his fate.

The changing of the guard

Spearheaded by U.S. President Reagan and U.K. Prime Minister Margaret Thatcher, by the mid-1980s, the neoliberal insurgency in economic policymaking was gathering momentum. Buoyed by their landslide re-elections, the Thatcher and Reagan governments grabbed the opportunity presented by a neophyte Secretary-General to accelerate the OECD's conversion to supply side doctrines that had begun in the 1970s (see Chapter 1). Paye's arrival in Paris was accompanied by a flurry of changes in senior OECD personnel, most conspicuously the appointment of David Henderson as head of the Economics Department and chief economist. Nominated for the post by Thatcher owing to his backing for her economic counterrevolution, Henderson used his position to impart neoliberal thinking to much of the Secretariat.[8]

Given its centrality to the subsequent OECD story and the implications for its operations, it is worth pausing to outline the main precepts of the neoliberal model. Distilled from numerous philosophical streams, neoliberalism is a notoriously slippery concept whose refraction through domestic policy processes has spawned endless national mutations.[9] Nevertheless, it is possible to discern a core set of premises and practices around which neoliberalism revolves. Neoliberalism borrows from neoclassical economic theories simplifying assumptions about economic agents and their motivations. This approach presents the economy as an assemblage of two types of rational actors: profit maximizing firms and utility maximizing households. Under conditions of perfect competition, the optimizing behavior of these rational agents will automatically lead to equilibrium levels of output and consumption. It therefore follows that economies, polities, and societies should be organized around competition provided via market mechanisms. Consequently, the role of the state should be confined to providing the institutional milieu in which competition can flourish by securing property rights, fixing market failures, and otherwise setting the framework for efficient market operations. From now on, the OECD's stencil for economic growth would be a diet of low taxes, flexible labor markets, aggressive liberalization of trade, finance and investment, balanced budgets, and public sector modernization.

The transition to neoliberalism altered the nature and content of OECD work. By the end of the 1980s, progressive or structural adjustment policies had superseded the synchronization of macroeconomic policies as the OECD's primary focus. This reflected the emerging credo that coordinated government tampering in macroeconomic matters was futile, or even counterproductive, because of the long run tendency of markets toward equilibrium. Continuing with this logic, the tribulations of the international economy were now believed to derive from flaws in domestic policy blueprints, not least structural rigidities arising from excessive state interference with the market mechanism. This inspired the establishment of EPC Working Party No. 1 on Macroeconomic and Structural Policy Analysis in 1980, plus a slew of publications identifying the distortions and rigidities hampering the economic performance of OECD countries. The results culminated in the OECD's capstone 1987 report *Structural Adjustment and Economic Performance*, which urged the adoption of market oriented reforms to consumer markets, the supply and allocation of factors of production and the discharge of the state's fiscal and regulatory responsibilities.[10] Subsequent MCM communiqués implored the OECD to strengthen analysis and surveillance of structural policies to mobilize peer pressure on states to eliminate obstacles to efficient market operations across a litany of areas.

This new reasoning came to suffuse the OECD's outputs and recommendations. Under the aegis of the Code of Liberalisation of Capital Movements and Code of Liberalisation of Invisible Operations signed in 1961, OECD countries had significantly relaxed restrictions on longer term foreign investment,[11] but fears about the destabilizing influence of 'hot money' had ensured short-term capital flows were excluded. Mounting faith in the self-equilibrating market, however, meant concerns about economic instability were outweighed by the alleged benefits of short-term capital flows. Led by the City of London and New York, the sweep of financial liberalization widened during the 1980s with many OECD countries reducing or eliminating exchange controls and opening their domestic financial markets to international competition. Accordingly in 1989, the OECD expanded the scope of its code on capital movements to incorporate short-term capital flows, thereby hardwiring financial liberalization into the identity of developed states. With adherence to the codes being "the most consequential obligation of OECD membership,"[12] the process of liberalization started by leading states in the organization would apply to its laggards and to any country hoping for OECD membership.

The OECD's work on labor, likewise became suffused with free market values. The 1992 MCM exhorted the OECD to undertake a "comprehensive research effort on the reasons for and the remedies to the disappointing progress in reducing unemployment."[13] The resulting OECD *Jobs Study* synthesized the secretariat's findings in labor adjustment, wage formation, trade, taxation, welfare, education, technology, and entrepreneurship. Anchored in neoclassical economic theory, the *Jobs Study* argued that raising employment required the removal of state intervention to produce more flexible labor markets. The 10 broad policy guidelines in the Jobs Study were subsequently translated into 45 more detailed recommendations as part of an OECD *Jobs Strategy*, whose implementation was monitored by the EDRC. Adoption of the OECD's recommendations was patchy; as was the evidence at they improved labor market performance.[14] Reassessed versions of the Jobs Strategy remain central to the OECD's work and the multidisciplinary approach underlying it would become an archetype for the organization's work in areas such as green growth.

Supporting wider global governance processes

After drifting apart in the early 1980s, structural issues also rekindled OECD-G7 relations. At the start of the decade, criticism from within the OECD Secretariat of the Reagan administration's monetarist policies fueled the United States' suspicion that the organization was too infatuated with Keynesianism to be entrusted with preparations for the G7 Summits.[15] The reconciliation of the OECD and G7 owed to the former's growing enthusiasm for free markets and the latter's need for evidence, analysis and surveillance of structural issues. Communiqués released after G7 summit and ministerial gatherings betrayed their mounting reliance on the OECD. In the third summit cycle (1989–95), communiqués made 37 references to the OECD and its work compared with 26 during the first two summit cycles (1975–88) combined (see Table 6.1). The G7-OECD relationship also changed qualitatively.

In the first two cycles, G7 communiqués vindicated the OECD's existing work but in the third cycle were more likely to urge greater efforts from the OECD or instruct it to investigate virgin terrain. Through the G7 the OECD also acquired new responsibilities, for example, becoming the base for the Financial Action Task Force (FATF), a body mandated by the G7 to tackle the scourge of money laundering and, later, financing of terrorism and the proliferation of weapons of mass destruction.

The OECD continued to be a forward-looking organization, undertaking the groundwork on topics such as ageing societies, biotechnology, anti-competitive practices, and cryptography. Often the analyses, frameworks, and recommendations of the OECD would become the basis of formal negotiation in other forums. Nothing illustrates this better than the OECD's environmental work. In the 1970s, the OECD began to collect data on the use of chlorofluorocarbons (CFCs) in response to concerns about stratospheric ozone depletion. The OECD's studies of the health impacts of CFCs, their effects on atmospheric processes, and the ramifications of alternative remedies to reduce CFC emissions bled into the negotiation of UNEP's 1987 Montreal Protocol on Substances That Deplete the Ozone Layer. Similarly, the OECD's work on shipments of hazardous wastes produced guidelines and principles that went on to form the nucleus of UNEP's 1989 Basel Convention on the Control of Transboundary Movements of Hazardous Wastes and their Disposal. The OECD was also an important contributor to formative work on the economics of climate change, divining the socio-economic implications of different tools and strategies for limiting greenhouse gas emissions. Another by-product of this was the OECD's pioneering work into the measurement of, and setting reporting parameters for, greenhouse emissions subsequently embraced by the Intergovernmental Panel on Climate Change.[16]

Finally, the OECD started to extend a hand more readily and regularly to non-members. The globalization of human activity bound the fate of OECD members to non-members that, until now, often featured only peripherally on the organization's radar. Despite exceptions such as the OECD Development Centre, where a number of developing countries had participated on an equal footing from the very beginning, non-members often did not have a seat at the table, even where they were a central concern, such as in the DAC. The Centre for Cooperation with European Economies in Transition and the Partners in Transition programme conveyed OECD acumen to the fledgling market democracies of Central and Eastern Europe.

Dialogue with the briskly growing markets of Asia and Latin America was conducted under the auspices of the Dynamic Non-Member Economies initiative. In 1995, this morphed into the Emerging Market Economy Forum, a more thematically based approach to non-member involvement. These various initiatives lubricated the accessions of Mexico (1994), the Czech Republic (1995), Hungary (1996), Poland (1996), South Korea (1996), and the Slovak Republic (2000).

Reinvention: Donald Johnston (1996–2006)

In 1994, Paye's petition for a third spell as secretary-general foundered on opposition from prominent member countries, most notably the United States. They insisted the organization needed incisive leadership that was more likely to be forthcoming from the appointment of Canada's Donald Johnston. A lawyer turned politician, Johnston held five different ministerial portfolios in the cabinets of Pierre Trudeau and John Turner (1980–84). An ardent advocate of free trade, he rebelled against his party to vote for the Canada-United States Free Trade Agreement in 1988. Retiring from Parliament shortly thereafter, he went on to be President of the Liberal Party (1990–94) whose leader and then Prime Minister, Jean Chretien, nominated him for the OECD hot seat. With the investiture of a Secretary-General requiring unanimity, however, Johnston's path was blocked by the incumbent's support amongst many continental European members. When Paye's term expired in September 1994 this standoff had not been resolved and Steffan Sohlman, Sweden's ambassador to the OECD, assumed temporary command. In November 1994, OECD members reluctantly accepted a Franco-Canadian compromise that extended Paye's reign until June 1996, after which Johnston would take the helm.

Johnston inherited a listless organization still fumbling around for a post-Cold War role. The OECD's exclusivity, once central to its comparative advantage, was increasingly a liability. In a globalizing world where non-members were exerting appreciable influence over economic, social, and environmental progress, discussing and formulating mechanisms to govern these matters in their absence appeared futile and illegitimate. When members sought restricted forums, regional organizations were tempting alternatives to the OECD. This was most pronounced among European members who were pouring diplomatic capital into expanding the competence and authority of what, since 1992, was the European Union (EU). The revitalization of universal international organizations, epitomized by the birth of the WTO, added to the institutional competition. The result was "diminished interest in capitals to make use of the OECD as a practical means to bring about institutional and policy change."[17] The 1996 MCM instructed the incoming Secretary-General to "accelerate the process of structural change......with a view to further enhancing the relevance, efficiency and effectiveness of the Organization."[18] Competing agendas frustrated rapid or revolutionary change nevertheless, Johnston's facelift prepared the way for more ambitious reforms under his successor.

OECD modernization

Armed with his modernization mandate, Johnston embarked on a three-pronged strategy involving internal rejigging, external outreach, and enlargement. An 18 percent fall in the real terms budget between 1996 and 1999[19] meant an internal overhaul of management and financial governance was essential if the OECD was to reconcile the member's desires for expansion with financial stringency. In 1996, an Executive Directorate was created to oversee the OECD's assets and work program. Through streamlining budgetary systems and introducing modern management practices, the Executive Directorate purged outlays by a fifth and realigned resources with the member's priorities.[20] To this end, the OECD also rationalized its committees and directorates. For example, education, previously clustered with labor and social affairs, acquired an independent directorate to satiate member demands for data to compare and benchmark education systems (see below). Similarly, financial and enterprise affairs were separated from fiscal matters, with the latter becoming the responsibility of the Centre for Tax Policy and Administration. These developments were supplemented by infrastructural improvements. The Online Information System (OLIS) put the OECD in the vanguard of experiments by international institutions with virtual technology and a new conference center was appended as part of an upgrade to the organization's headquarters.

Responsibility for outreach became the responsibility of a new Centre for Cooperation with Non-Members (CCNM). Created in 1998, the CCNM subsumed the OECD's disparate liaisons with non-members and became the lynchpin of what later blossomed into the OECD's Global Relations Strategy (see Chapter 6). Most importantly, the CCNM chaperoned tailored programmes of dialogue and cooperation with large non-member countries including the Russian Federation, China, and Brazil. Another dimension of outreach concerned civil society. The turning point was the OECD's abortive attempt to negotiate the Multilateral Agreement on Investment (MAI). After similar initiatives in the WTO foundered on opposition from capital importing countries, the MAI was designed to be a binding treaty that ensured the equitable treatment of domestic and foreign investment. Ultimately, the MAI was doomed by dissent among OECD members about the agreement's scope, effects on sovereign authority and concerns that it would inhibit their flexibility in future WTO investment negotiations.[21] The collapse of the negotiations would probably have garnered little attention had it not been for the virulent opposition of civil society. Condemning the proposals as an "investor's charter, privileging the pursuit of profit and eviscerating the ability of governments to pass legislation to protect customers, workers and the environment,"[22] the anti-MAI campaign involved over 600 groups from 70 countries[23] climaxing with two days of direct action in Paris in October 1998. Civil society did not capsize the MAI, but the attendant commotion and consternation that anti-globalization sentiment could scupper future initiatives, spooked the OECD into action. Led by the Public Affairs Directorate created in 1997, measures to enrich OECD-civil society relations were a mixture of showpiece events, such as the Annual Forum (see Chapter 3), and improvements to the OECD's communication with, and accessibility to, the public.

Enlargement, the final tranche of Johnson's reforms, was the most contentious. Quarrels about the pace, direction, sequence, and extent of expansion and its impact on the OECD's temperament led to the deputation of a Working Group on the Enlargement Strategy. Their deliberations, distilled into a report commended by the 2004 MCM, delineated the criterion for aspirant members (see Chapter 6). This cleared the way for the OECD to open accession pathways for Chile, Estonia, Israel, Slovenia, and the Russian Federation in 2007.

OECD work

As ever, the ambiguity of its Convention meant the OECD was the victim and the beneficiary of forum shopping. The advent of the WTO downgraded the organization's role in the trade sphere. Agricultural and services trade, once core OECD concerns, now fell within the WTO's purview while its Trade Policy Review Mechanism usurped OECD surveillance of the global trade system. Likewise, with the WTO affording ample opportunities to meet their OECD counterparts and also non-OECD countries that many trade deadlocks now involved, senior trade officials seldom graced the Trade Committee. Regardless, the WTO continued to make use of the OECD's research and analytical tools, and the two secretariats began to work closely on technical assistance and capacity building in developing countries.[24]

Conversely, in education and health, the OECD profited from the travails of institutional competitors. Traditionally, the OECD's education work focused predominantly on the inputs to education systems but with the onset of neoliberalism, OECD members became more inquisitive about their outputs. Specifically, they were curious about the relative performance of their education systems in equipping citizens, and by extension their economies, with the skills to compete in the global economy. The OECD found itself vying with UNESCO for the privilege of housing a programme to generate internationally comparable data to assess the quality of national education systems. Owing to concerns over the running of UNESCO and the project becoming hostage to its developing country majority, members plumped for the OECD, which duly launched the Programme for International Student Assessment (PISA) in 1997. Using standardized tests and survey questionnaires, PISA measured and ranked the reading, mathematical, and scientific competences of those about to leave compulsory schooling and was the forerunner for a smorgasbord of activities related to "lifelong learning for all," an overarching framework adopted by a 1996 meeting of OECD education ministers.[25] PISA exemplified the power of international benchmarking (see Chapter 4), with a mediocre showing sometimes startling domestic publics and policymakers into mobilizing behind educational reform.[26] The creation of a dedicated Directorate for Education (EDU), cleaved from the Directorate for Employment, Labour and Social Affairs (DELSA) in 2002, signposted education's transition from having only an "inferred role"[27] at the OECD to one that was central to its portfolio.

Like education, discussions of health at the OECD dated to the 1950s but as adjuncts to other concerns. From the 1970s, the OECD refined data and purveyed a steady stream of studies on healthcare expenditures. In the 1990s, the attention of OECD countries switched to wringing better performances from their healthcare systems in a context where clinical advances and aging societies could otherwise see costs spiral out of control. Annoyance at the feeble showing of their healthcare systems in World Health Organization (WHO) survey and the dexterity of the secretary-general in touting the organization's pre-existing expertise prompted members to breathe new life into the health dossier. Running from 2001 to 2004 and involving four directorates, the OECD Health Project measured and explained variations in health system performance. The programme resulted in a step-change in the quality and availability of internationally comparable indicators of health care outcomes and sponsored the emergence of the OECD Health Committee in 2007.

Faithful to the Convention, the OECD's work still germinated from a fixation with economic growth. Under the tutelage of neoliberalism, the state's role in OECD economies was shifting from direct intervention to the regulation of market exchanges. Much of the OECD's work was devoted to filling out a template for the ideal "regulatory state."[28] The amalgamation of the Public Management Directorate and the Territorial Development Service into the Directorate for Public Governance and Territorial Development reflected the OECD members' thirst for consolidating the modernization of public administrations to ensure good governance and optimize their capacity to instigate, organize, and implement efficient and effective regulatory reforms.[29] Elsewhere, the OECD acted as a pathfinder for emergent regulatory problems. For instance, recognizing the challenges of rapid technological developments, the Directorate for Science, Technology and Innovation elaborated recommendations to protect consumers conducting e-commerce (1999), the security of information systems and networks (2002), broadband development (2003), and the licensing of genetic inventions (2005). The Asian financial crisis of 1997–98 spurred the OECD Principles of Corporate Governance. The first intergovernmental accord on corporate governance, the Principles became part of the then Financial Stability Forum's (FSF's) 12 Key Standards for Sound Financial Systems and the World Bank/IMF Reports on the Observance of Standards and Codes. On a related theme, the OECD Convention on Combating Bribery of Foreign Public Officials in International Business Transactions, a rare case of OECD 'hard' law entering into force in 1999, was followed a year later by a fourth revision of the Declaration on International Investment and Multinational Enterprises.

At the 1998 MCM "support was also given to re-interpret Article 1 of the OECD Convention such that the term 'sustainable' as applied to economic growth includes social and environmental considerations"[30] and environment ministers conscripted the OECD to formulate an environmental strategy for the 2000s. Confirming sustainable development as a strategic priority for the OECD the strategy, endorsed by the 2001 MCM, identified 71 actions for states to take to secure sustainable development. To encourage implementation, the OECD redoubled surveillance, devising pristine indicators to measure progress and adding sections on environmental sustainability to its *Economic Surveys*. The OECD also became more embroiled in the preparation and follow-up activities of a string of international conferences, most notably those associated with the UNFCCC. In parallel with economic well-being and social development, environmental sustainability was a key theme in the MDG's, another initiative prefaced by work at the OECD. A 1994 DAC meeting concluded that adopting concrete targets for development policy would help to counter aid fatigue among skeptical donor publics by raising awareness of global poverty and the progress made by development cooperation in eradicating it. Over the next two years, the DAC boiled down the international community's multiplicity of development targets into seven goals[31] that, propagated by key messengers and not without controversy,[32] became the core MDGs.

The OECD's sweeping policy repertoire reinforced its relationship with what was now the G8. References to the OECD in G8 communiqués jumped almost fivefold in the fourth cycle of meetings (1996–2002) and by a further 25 percent in the fifth cycle (2003–10). The G8's continued fascination with structural issues gave impulses to OECD work on ageing societies, bribery, biotechnology, food safety, corporate governance, regulatory reform, development, education, environment, health, and investment. It also propelled another aspect of OECD work that would become critical to the organization's twenty-first century relevance, the promotion of international tax transparency.

Starting in 1977, the OECD's Working Party on Tax Avoidance and Evasion had amassed evidence of national exchequers hemorrhaging tax revenues owing to wealthy citizens and corporations parking their assets "offshore." This was being facilitated by the interplay between financial liberalization and fiscal regimes deliberately designed to lure mobile capital by offering an environment that combined low or no rates of taxation with secrecy provisions or opaque corporate structures that protected assets from the privations of tax inspectors overseas. In 1996, the G7 labeled this "harmful tax competition" and "strongly urged the OECD to vigorously pursue its work in this field."[33] All OECD countries bar Switzerland and Luxembourg endorsed the organization's 1998 Recommendation on Counteracting Harmful Tax Competition, obliging them to improve the transparency of their tax regimes and the exchange of information with foreign tax authorities within five years. Contentiously the OECD agreed that 41 non-member "tax havens" must make equivalent commitments or face "countermeasures" from its members. Non-members, abetted by the transnational tax planning industry, pushed back successfully against the initiative by questioning its legitimacy and pointing out it contravened widely held norms, not least the sovereign prerogative of states to set their own tax laws and the OECD's views about the value of competition.[34] Graver challenges arose in 2001 when the United States withdrew support for key parts of the project. The OECD kept the project alive by pledging that the imposition of penalties against non-members would commence only after they applied to members and tapering the definition of 'harmful' tax practices. The first indulgence rendered the OECD recommendation "virtually meaningless"[35] because it could not be enforced without Switzerland and Luxembourg signing up, something they were loath to do. Narrowing its agenda to focus on developing a conceptual and legal framework for the exchange of information between tax authorities, the OECD soldiered on. Its time was about to come.

Redemption? Angel Gurria (2006–21)

The former Secretary of Foreign Affairs (1994–97) and Finance and Public Credit (1998–2000) of Mexico, Angel Gurria, took office as secretary-general in June 2006. The first secretary-general from outside the founding OECD countries, his appointment reflected the member's enthusiasm for his pitch to implement a more assertive reform strategy to reposition the organization and re-establish its centrality to a core of global governance functions. Disagreements between leading members and a decade long real terms budget freeze took their toll toward the end of his stint. Nevertheless, Gurria was an energetic and entrepreneurial secretary-general who galvanized significant change, leaving behind an organization better able to acquit itself in a globalized world.

The 2008 global financial crisis was the defining moment of Gurria's term. The reverberations from this event could easily have hobbled OECD reform. Instead, Gurria skillfully exploited the crisis, using it as an opportunity to peddle the OECD's wares in national capitals and international institutions and drive organizational change. First, the 2008 crisis was the latest in a series of escalating economic emergencies in which the neoliberal paradigm championed by the OECD was cited as the chief culprit.[36] Recognizing the need to temper the excesses of unbridled capitalism, the OECD reappraised its growth narrative. Encapsulated in the motto "better policies for better lives"[37] adopted at the OECD's 50th anniversary, the OECD would henceforth look "beyond growth,"[38] complementing GDP metrics with consideration of whether economic growth was inclusive, green and contributed to human well-being. Second, distancing the OECD from its incarnation as a "think tank," Gurria rebranded the organization as a "do tank"[39] whose accomplishments actively responded to, and advanced the interests of, its patrons. Under the heading "going national," the OECD sought to tailor general toolkits to the specific challenges of individual countries. New products including the *Better Policies* and *Getting it Right* series, the latter aimed specifically at incoming administrations, were directed at enabling governments to bring reform agendas to fruition. Finally, as Chapter 6 discusses, the OECD's go national agenda was paralleled by an attempt to go global. The member's resolution "to make the OECD a more effective and inclusive global policy network"[40] and strengthen its global character emboldened the earlier enlargement and engagement initiatives. The accessions of Chile, Estonia, Israel, and Slovenia in 2010 were followed by Latvia (2016), Lithuania (2018), Colombia (2020), and Costa Rica (2021). Redoubling efforts to engage with a wider variety of non-members (see also, Chapter 3), the OECD intensified and institutionalized its relationship with the G20. By engaging with emerging non-member countries in the G20, the OECD embroidered its reputation as an organization to which the investigations of leading global economic challenges could be devolved. Enlargement and growing entanglements with non-members, including civil society and states outside the G20, however, brought fresh challenges for the OECD's governance and identity (see Chapter 6).

"Beyond growth": A new paradigm?

The "Great Moderation,"[41] a moniker bestowed upon the relatively long period of stable, low inflationary growth until 2007, lent credence to the neoliberal model, and the view that business cycle had been tamed by the institutional and structural changes undertaken at the behest, amongst others, of the OECD. This was called into question by the emanation of a crisis in the heartland of global capitalism whose cause, in Gurria's words "was created by the system itself, the system which we created; and by a toxic combination of unethical behavior by companies and a faulty regulation and supervision of their activities."[42] The liberal DNA coursing through the OECD's genes made it reluctant to forswear market-oriented solutions, but the crisis did spark reflection about shortcomings in the organization's analytical frameworks.

Launched at the 2012 MCM, the New Approaches to Economic Challenges (NAEC) initiative was tasked with diagnosing the causes and drawing lessons from the crisis as a basis for revising the OECD's analytical frameworks and policy advice.[43] Reflecting the changes underway in the OECD's reasoning, NAEC's final synthesis report suggested that quantitative economic growth, normally viewed as an end, should be conceived as a means to enhance the well-being of people and the planet. To mirror the complexity of globalization and the economy's synergies with society and the environment, NAEC favored analyzing the global economy as a "complex adaptive system."[44] Incorporating insights from other disciplines and coordinating projects on planetary emergencies, neuroeconomics, econophysics, systems thinking, and resilience, the second phase of NAEC activity involved leeching these insights into mainstream OECD analysis.

Throughout the 2010s, the "beyond growth" narrative was increasingly felt across the OECD. The 2009 MCM requested the OECD develop a Green Growth Strategy.[45] Unveiled in 2011, the strategy elucidated a framework for countries at different levels of development to pursue economic growth in a manner compatible with combating climate change and avoiding the depletion of natural assets.[46] That this initiative incorporated attempts to mitigate any regressive effects of the shift to green policies spoke to the OECD's worries about sharp rises in inequality.[47] Beginning in 2012, the Inclusive Growth initiative aimed to ensure that governments were equipped with the data and policy advice necessary to ensure the fruits of economic growth and the opportunities to contribute to it were spread more evenly. The measure of "multidimensional living standards" introduced by the OECD's 2014 Framework for Inclusive Growth recognized, alongside income, the many non-material aspects to inequality and non-material factors contributing to social progress.[48] This dovetailed with an intensification of OECD work on well-being. The preamble to the OECD Convention talks of the determination of governments to "improve the economic and social well-being of their peoples."[49] Intermittent attempts by the OECD to define well-being or related notions such as the "quality of life" and to develop indicators to gauge it date to the 1971 Social Indicators Programme.[50] Resuscitated in 1998 by a Social Policy Ministerial, the OECD was part of a wider zeitgeist that questioned whether traditional macroeconomic statistics such as GDP were satisfactory proxies for well-being. In 2011, this work became part of the OECD's Better Life Initiative. Informed by the OECD Framework for Measuring Wellbeing and Progress, the regular publication *How's Life* uses 80 indicators to monitor well-being trends in 41 countries while the *Better Life Index* provides an interactive tool that allows users to compare well-being performance of countries across 11 dimensions. The creation in 2020 of a dedicated directorate, the OECD Centre on Well-being, Inclusion, Sustainability and Equal Opportunity, conveys the centrality of well-being to the organization's remit.

Another arrow in this quiver was the OECD's Skills Strategy unveiled at the 2012 MCM.[51] Overseen by the rebadged Directorate for Education and Skills, the Skills Strategy underpinned a rapid expansion in the OECD's educational universe. With 87 jurisdictions in its 2022 iteration, the number of PISA participants has doubled since the turn of the century. Starting in 2013, the PISA for Development (PISA-D) initiative aims to facilitate the involvement of lower and middle-income countries in PISA. PISA-D's evolution coincided with the OECD's participation in the UNESCO led effort to define a post-MDG agenda for education. Assisted by the World Bank,[52] the OECD ensured that the Sustainable Development Goal (SDG) for education contained a not only a quantitative dimension (ensuring all children completed free primary and secondary education) but also a qualitative dimension (that it should lead to "relevant and effective learning outcomes"[53]), interposing PISA-D as an instrument to audit progress against the latter.[54] PISA was also the prototype for a suite of projects to measure lifelong learning including the Programme for the International Assessment of Adult Competencies (PIAAC) and Assessment of Higher Education Learning Outcomes.[55] Away from formal education systems, the OECD turned its attention to the quantification of other attributes contributing to human capital and innovation including problem solving skills, behavioral traits, and cognitive competencies.[56]

Whether all this amounts to a rupture in OECD analysis is more questionable. After 2008, the OECD's affection for fiscal stimulus and intervention in financial markets soon cooled. Led by the Economics Department (ECO), the OECD became an enthusiastic proponent of austerity policies.[57] Despite austerity aggravating inequality, stalling well-being improvements, and shrinking the public sphere so indispensable to democratic politics,[58] the OECD's coronavirus response borrows from the same playbook (see Chapter 5). Ultimately, the OECD's turn to inclusive and green economies derives from habitual concerns, namely how inequality and resource depletion might detract from economic growth, productivity and competitiveness. Flagship programmes such as the Jobs Strategy, whose third incarnation appeared at the 2018 MCM[59], exemplify the continuity in the OECD's mentality. While name checking inclusivity and the need for high quality employment, by placing this in a context of globalizing world in which labor must adjust to rapid technological change and intense competition, the new Jobs Strategy resembles its forebears. Nods toward better working conditions, social dialogue, and worker protection are drowned out by the familiar drumbeat of labor market flexibility. By ignoring how current labor market circumstances have been shaped by the implementation of policies backed by the OECD or the possibility of alternative governance strategies capable of blunting the effects of globalization the Jobs Strategy "limits its policy recommendations to those consistent with the adaptation to, rather than control over, actually existing markets."[60]

Globalizing OECD governance

In its heyday, the OECD's guidelines often became *de facto* global standards by virtue of the member's weight in the world economy. As their dominance receded, so did the relevance and legitimacy of these standards prompting the organization to find new ways to roll OECD governance out globally. Alongside direct liaison with non-member states, the OECD has used the G20 as an interface for strategic engagement with the rising powers of the Global South. OECD-G20 relations got off to a sticky start, with the emerging powers wary of welcoming inputs or the participation of delegates from an organization ostensibly representing the developed world. The perseverance of the Secretary-General won over these opponents and the OECD-G20 nexus has prospered (see Chapter 6).

Like with the G7/8, and often in cooperation with other international organizations, the OECD leverages its expertise to provide policy narratives and options for a plethora of subjects that come before the G20. Seizing the moment to globalize OECD governance, the organization has sought to ensure that existing OECD guidelines have become the fulcrum of G20 responses on bribery and corruption and AI and offered to work together with G20 countries to revise or define new joint standards such as the G20/OECD Principles of Corporate Governance (2015) and the G20 High-Level Principles of Long-Term Investment Financing by Institutional Investors (2014) and Quality Infrastructure Investment (2019). The OECD is also a valuable source of surveillance for the G20, providing oversight of progress toward the implementation of specific commitments and encouraging countries to embrace the structural policies needed to thrive in a globalized world. Occasionally, as in the case of the Global Forum on Steel Excess Capacity, this has required new institutional machinery. Established in response to the 2016 Hangzhou Summit the forum, facilitated by the OECD, provides a mechanism for countries to exchange information about capacity in the industry, government policies in relation to it, and seek principles to ease the overabundance of steel entering the global market.[61]

Taxation, however, is the issue that most contributed to the OECD-G20's maturing relationship. Aided initially by the opportunism of Angel Gurria (see Chapter 6), the G20 prioritized reform of the international tax architecture thereby resurrecting the OECD's seemingly moribund tax transparency agenda. The watershed moment was the 2009 London Summit where the G20 pledged "to take action against non-cooperative jurisdictions"[62] named on an updated list of non-compliant jurisdictions from the OECD's Global Forum on Transparency and Exchange of Information. Newly in possession of its own secretariat, the Forum was restructured as a venue where all countries could meet on an equal footing to negotiate and review progress in implementing standards to promote the exchange of tax information. Standing at 163 members in December 2021, the Global Forum has dampened some of the criticism about the legitimacy of OECD's tax work and exemplifies the way in which the organization is increasingly a node in global governance networks.

Jurisdictions rushed to enact the OECD standard requiring them to sign deals to exchange information about the assets of non-residents on request from foreign tax authorities. Derided as a weak reed, the standard did little to deter tax avoidance and evasion.[63] The problems were manifold, but the biggest was the standard's reliance on voluntary exchange of information. Before a national tax authority could request information on a citizen's foreign assets, they needed to know of their existence, precisely the thing that tax haven secrecy precludes. Nonetheless, the OECD was unperturbed eyeing voluntary exchange of information as a waypoint to forge consensus behind a standard based on the automatic exchange of information (AEOI).

Involving the "systematic and periodic transmission of 'bulk' taxpayer information,"[64] AEOI is a more powerful weapon as it can help to detect non-compliance with tax laws even where revenue authorities have no prior inkling of it. The advocacy of AEOI by the UN Stiglitz Commission, its implementation in the EU Savings Tax Directive and the passage of the United States' Foreign Account Tax Compliance Act, obliging foreign financial institutions to identify and report accounts belonging to US tax residents, evinced accumulating political support for its adoption as the international standard. In September 2013, the G20 Summit "committed to automatic exchange of information as the new standard" and asked the OECD to develop a uniform framework to facilitate it. Issued in 2014, the OECD's Common Reporting Standard, to which 112 jurisdictions were committed in November 2021[65], became the basis for AEOI, a process that began in earnest in 2017 (see Chapter 5).

The G20 also oxygenated parallel OECD work on corporate tax avoidance. Manipulating rules designed in the 1920s, multinational enterprises were lowering their tax bills by creating artificial schisms between the place where economic value was added and the profits from those activities were declared for tax purposes.[66] Responding to G20 requests[67], and building on its existing work, in 2013 the OECD delivered its *Base Erosion and Profit Shifting* (BEPS) report outlining 15 areas for study.[68] The final reports on these areas published in 2015 led to a compendium of recommendations including four BEPS minimum standards to combat harmful tax practices, counter tax treaty abuse, instigate Country-by-Country reporting, and improve resolution of tax disputes between jurisdictions. They also flagged the areas requiring additional work, for example, on tax challenges arising from the digital economy (see Chapter 5). To further this initiative, the OECD, acting on another G20 mandate[69], opened its Committee on Fiscal Affairs to interested jurisdictions to create the OECD/G20 Inclusive Framework on BEPS in 2016. Premised on principles similar to the Global Forum on Transparency, the Inclusive Framework is a place where 141 countries (as of November 2021) advance the debate on BEPS and monitor compliance with international standards. Its key achievements include the conclusion of negotiations on the Multilateral Convention to Implement Tax Treaty Related Measures to Prevent Base Erosion and Profit Shifting (MLI). Signed by 95 countries,[70] this instrument modifies tax treaty measures that help to implement the BEPS minimum standards and reduce instances of tax avoidance by multinational companies.

Conclusion: Postscript Mathias Cormann (2021—?)

For over seven decades, the OEEC and OECD have worked furtively in the ongoing drama of global governance. If global governance had an Oscar ceremony, rarely would either organization have been nominated as the leading thespian. Nevertheless, they would have amassed a horde of gongs for "best supporting actor" in major productions such as the Uruguay Round trade negotiations, the MDGs, and the G7/8/20 summits. Furthermore, through their data, concepts, and analysis, the OEEC and OECD have scripted the dialogue and stitched the costumes of the protagonists. At other times, the OEEC and OECD have designed and provided the stage on which actors have performed. Indeed, the OECD is the leading, and in many cases, the only source of international rules governing a swathe of issues. Hovering in the wings, the organization has calmed cantankerous artistes, frequently using the Chateau de la Muette as a citadel where feuding parties could retreat to repair relationships otherwise likely to delay or torpedo the overall production.

Nonetheless, when in July 2020 Gurria notified OECD ambassadors that he would not court reappointment, formidable challenges lay in wait for his successor. Alongside orchestrating the response to the coronavirus crisis (see Chapter 5), the incoming secretary-general faces a wavering reform process (see Chapter 6) and an unpropitious geo-political backdrop (see Chapter 7). Through the usual selection process, the ten candidates nominated for the post by member states were winnowed out, resulting in Mathias Cormann becoming the sixth OECD secretary-general in June 2021. Born in Belgium and later emigrating to Australia where he served as Minister for Finance (2013–2020), Cormann's European heritage combined with his Asia-Pacific connections epitomes the organization he fronts. Citing his record in government and skeptical statements on climate change, environmental groups reacted with dismay to his appointment. During his campaign, Cormann backtracked on many of these comments and used his first speech as secretary-general to call on the OECD to "drive and promote global leadership on ambitious and effective action on climate change to achieve global net-zero emissions by 2050."[71] Nothing in his vision statement for the organization suggests a dramatic departure from the past. In it Cormann promises to head an OECD that is

> "the world's centre of excellence for credible, evidence-based economic analysis, advice and policy guidance; focused on members' needs and true to members' shared democratic values of opportunity, prosperity and stability for all; a strong advocate of economic openness, transparency and international rules and standards; and engaged with all the world's regions, including the Asia-Pacific."[72]

The explicit reference to the Asia-Pacific aside, this manifesto could have been written by any of the OECD's secretary-generals.

Notes

1 Edward Luttwak, *Turbo-Capitalism: Winners and Losers in the Global Economy* (New York: HarperCollins, 1999).

2 Wolfgang Streeck, *Buying Time: The Delayed Crisis of Democratic Capitalism (2nd edition)* (London: Verso, 2017); Adam Tooze, *How a Decade of Financial Crisis Changed the World* (London: Penguin, 2019).

3 Robert Wolfe, "From Reconstructing Europe to Constructing Globalization: the OECD in Historical Perspective," in *The OECD and Transnational Governance*, eds. Rianne Mahon and Stephen McBride (Vancouver: UBC Press, 2008), 28.
4 Rianne Mahon, "In Conversation with Ron Gass: The OECD and the Crisis of Progress," *Global Social Policy* 15, no. 2 (2015): 113–24.
5 OECD, *Getting to Grips with Globalisation: The OECD in a Changing World* (OECD: Paris, 2004).
6 Angel Gurria, "Ensuring a Smoother Flight," *OECD Observer* no. 264/5 (2007–8): 3.
7 Jean-Claude Paye, "OECD: Analyst and Catalyst," *OECD Observer* no. 44 (1987): 4–7.
8 Martin Wolf, "David Henderson, Economist, 1927–2018," *Financial Times* 9 October 2018, https://www.ft.com/content/ac700a10-c677-11e8-ba8f-ee390057b8c9; Samuel Beroud, ""Positive Adjustments": The Emergence of Supply-Side Economics in the OECD and G7, 1970–1984," in *The OECD and the International Political Economy Since 1948*, eds. Matthieu Leimgruber and Matthias Schmelzer (Basingstoke: Palgrave, 2017), 251–52.
9 See Dieter Plehwe, Quinn Slobodian and Philip Mirowski eds., *Nine Lives of Neoliberalism* (London: Verso, 2020).
10 OECD, *Structural Adjustment and Economic Performance* (OECD: Paris, 1987).
11 David Henderson, "The Role of the OECD in Liberalising International Trade and Capital Flows," *The World Economy* 19, no. 1 (1996): 15–21.
12 Rawi Abdelal, "Writing the Rules of Global Finance: France, Europe, and Capital Liberalization," *Review of International Political Economy* 13, no. 1 (2006): 1–27.
13 OECD, "Meeting of the Council at Ministerial Level in May 1992 Communiqué," http://www.g8.utoronto.ca/oecd/oecd92.htm.
14 Stephen McBride and Russell A. Williams, "Globalization, the Restructuring of Labour Markets and Policy Convergence," *Global Social Policy* 1, no. 3 (2001): 281–309.
15 Robert Putnam and Nicholas Bayne, *Hanging Together: Cooperation and Conflict in the Seven-Power Summits (2nd edition)* (London: Sage, 1987), 161; Samuel Beroud, ""Positive Adjustments": The Emergence of Supply-Side Economics in the OECD and G7, 1970–1984," 258.
16 Bill L. Long, *International Environmental Issues and the OECD 1950-2000* (Paris: OECD, 2000), 60–79.
17 OECD, *A Strategy for Enlargement and Outreach* (Paris: OECD, 2004), 7.
18 OECD, "Meeting of the Council at Ministerial Level Paris, 21–22 May 1996," http://www.g8.utoronto.ca/oecd/oecd96.htm.
19 OECD, *Council at Ministerial Level, 29–30 April 2003: Reform and Modernisation of the OECD*, C/MIN(2003)6, 7.
20 OECD, *Getting to Grips with Globalisation*, 27; Jocelyne Bourgon, *Reform and Modernisation of the OECD*, The Centre for International Governance Innovation Working Paper No. 42, May 2009, 6–9, 11–13.
21 Tony Hinton, "International Negotiations on Investment Liberalization," *Australian Journal of International Affairs* 57, no. 2 (2003): 253–58.

22 Richard Woodward, "The Organisation for Economic Cooperation and Development," *New Political Economy* 9, no. 1 (2004): 120.
23 Stephen J. Kobrin, "The MAI and the Clash of Globalizations," *Foreign Policy* no. 112 (1998), 97.
24 Robert Wolfe, "The OECD Contribution to the Evolution of Twenty-First Century Trade-Law," *Washington International Law Review* 43, no. 2 (2011): 290–93.
25 OECD, *Lifelong Learning for All: Meeting of the Education Committee at Ministerial Level, 16–17 January 1996* (Paris: OECD, 1996).
26 Sotiria Grek, "Governing by Numbers: The PISA 'Effect' in Europe," *Journal of Education Policy* 24, no. 1 (2009): 23–37.
27 George S. Papadopoulos, *Education 1960-1990: The OECD Perspective* (Paris: OECD, 1994), 11.
28 Giandomenico Majone, "From the Positive to the Regulatory State: Causes and Consequences of Changes in the Mode of Governance," *Journal of European Public Policy* 17, no. 2 (1997): 139–67.
29 Leslie Pal, *Frontiers of Governance: The OECD and Global Public Management Reform* (Basingstoke: Palgrave, 2012), 78–80.
30 OECD, *TUAC Evaluation of the Communiqué of the Meeting of the OECD Council at Ministerial Level, 27–28 April 1998*, PAC/AFF(98)1, 6.
31 OECD DAC, *Shaping the 21st Century: The Contribution of Development Co-operation* (Paris: OECD, 1996), 8–11.
32 Sakiko Fukuda-Parr and David Hulme, "International Norm Dynamics and the "End of Poverty": Understanding the Millennium Development Goals," *Global Governance* 17, no. 1 (2011): 17–36.
33 G7, "Economic Communiqué: Making a Success of Globalization for the Benefit of All,", 28 June 1996, http://www.g7.utoronto.ca/summit/1996lyon/communique.html.
34 Michael C. Webb, "Defining the Boundaries of Legitimate State Practice: Norms, Transnational Actors and the OECD's Project on Harmful Tax Competition," *Review of International Political Economy* 11, no. 4 (2004): 787–827; Jason Sharman, *Havens in a Storm: The Struggle for Global Tax Regulation* (Ithaca, N.Y.: Cornell University Press, 2006).
35 Woodward, "The Organisation for Economic Cooperation and Development," 119.
36 Paul Krugman, *The Return of Depression Economics* (London: Penguin, 2008).
37 OECD, *OECD 50th Anniversary Vision Statement*, C/MIN(2011)6FINAL, 17 June 2011, 2.
38 OECD, *Beyond Growth: Towards a New Economic Approach* (Paris: OECD, 2020).
39 OECD, *2019 Strategic Orientations of the Secretary-General*, C/MIN(2019)1, 2.
40 OECD, *OECD 50th Anniversary Vision Statement*, 2.
41 Federal Reserve Board, "Remarks by Governor Ben S. Bernanke At the meetings of the Eastern Economic Association, Washington, DC," 20 February 2004, https://www.federalreserve.gov/boarddocs/speeches/2004/20040220/.
42 Angel Gurria, "Business Ethics and OECD Principles: What Can be Done to Avoid Another Crisis," speech at the European Business

Ethics Forum 22 January 2009, https://www.oecd.org/economy/businessethicsandoecdprincipleswhatcanbedonetoavoidanothercrisis.htm.

43 OECD, *New Approaches to Economic Challenges – A Framework Paper*, C/MIN(2012)2/FINAL, 13 June 2012.

44 OECD, *Final NAEC Synthesis New Approaches to Economic Challenges* (Paris: OECD, 2015), 21.

45 OECD, *Declaration on Green Growth*, C/MIN(2009)5/ADD/FINAL, 25 June 2009.

46 OECD, *Towards Green Growth* (Paris: OECD, 2011).

47 OECD, *Growing Unequal? Income Distribution and Poverty in OECD Countries* (Paris: OECD, 2008).

48 OECD, *Report on the OECD Framework for Inclusive Growth* (Paris: OECD, 2014).

49 OECD, *Convention on the Organisation for Economic Co-operation and Development* (Paris: OECD, 1960).

50 Matthias Schmelzer, *The Hegemony of Growth: The OECD and the Making of the Economic Growth Paradigm* (Cambridge: Cambridge University Press, 2016), 300–12.

51 OECD, *Better Skills. Better Jobs. Better Lives. A Strategic Approach to Skills Policies* (Paris: OECD, 2012).

52 Euan Auld, Jeremy Rappleye and Paul Morris, "PISA for Development: how the OECD and World Bank shaped education governance post-2015," *Comparative Education* 55, no. 2 (2019): 197–219.

53 United Nations, "Sustainable Development Goal 4 Quality Education," https://www.un.org/sustainabledevelopment/education/.

54 Camilla Addey, "Golden Relics & Historical Standards: How the OECD is Expanding Global Education Governance through PISA for Development," *Critical Studies in Education* 58, no. 3 (2017): 321.

55 Sam Sellar and Bob Lingard, "The OECD and the Expansion of PISA: New Global Modes of Governance in Education," *British Educational Research Journal* 40, no. 6 (2014): 924–30.

56 OECD, *The Innovation Imperative: Contributing to Productivity, Growth and Well-Being* (Paris: OECD, 2015), 47–68.

57 Stephen McBride and Jessica Merolli, "Alternatives to Austerity: Post-crisis Policy Advice from Global Institutions," *Global Social Policy* 13, no. 3 (2013): 304–07.

58 Armin Schafer and Wolfgang Streeck (eds.), *Politics in the Age of Austerity* (Cambridge: Polity, 2013); Bryan M. Evans and Stephen McBride (eds.), *Austerity the Lived Experience* (Toronto: University of Toronto Press, 2017); Joseph E. Stiglitz, *Globalization and Its Discontents Revisited: Anti-Globalization in the Era of Trump* (New York: W.W. Norton & Company 2017).

59 OECD, *Good Jobs for All in a Changing World of Work: The OECD Jobs Strategy* (Paris: OECD, 2018).

60 Stephen McBride and James Watson, "Reviewing the 2018 OECD Jobs Strategy – Anything New Under the Sun?," *Transfer: European Review of Labour and Research* 25, no. 2 (2019): 160.

61 OECD, "Global Forum on Steel Excess Capacity," steelforum.org.

62 G20, "London Summit – Leaders' Statement 2 April 2009," http://www.g20.utoronto.ca/2009/2009communique0402.pdf.

63 Markus Meinzer, "The Creeping Futility of the Global Forum's Peer Reviews," *Tax Justice Network Briefing March 2012*, https://taxjustice.net/wp-content/uploads/2020/11/Global-Forum-2012-Creeping-Futility-TJN-Briefing-1.pdf.
64 OECD, *Automatic Exchange of Information: What It Is, How It Works, Benefits, What Remains to be Done?* (Paris: OECD, 2012), 7.
65 OECD, *Signatories of the Multilateral Competent Authority Agreement on Automatic Exchange of Financial Account Information and Intended First Information Exchange Date*, https://www.oecd.org/tax/exchange-of-tax-information/crs-mcaa-signatories.pdf.
66 Sol Picciotto, *International Business Taxation: A Study in the Internationalization of Business Regulation* (Cambridge: Cambridge University Press, 1992), 117–229.
67 G20, "G20 Leaders Declaration," 19 June 2012, http://www.g20.utoronto.ca/2012/2012-0619-loscabos.html.
68 OECD, *Addressing Base Erosion and Profit Shifting* (Paris: OECD, 2013).
69 G20, "G20 Leaders' Communiqué," 16 November 2015, http://www.g20.utoronto.ca/2015/151116-communique.html.
70 OECD, *Signatories and Parties to the Multilateral Convention to Implement Tax Treaty Related Measures to Prevent Base Erosion and Profit Shifting – Status as of 8 June 2021*, https://www.oecd.org/tax/treaties/beps-mli-signatories-and-parties.pdf.
71 Mathias Cormann, "Meeting of the OECD Council at Ministerial Level (MCM), Introductory Remarks by Mathias Cormann, 1 June 2021," https://www.oecd.org/about/secretary-general/oecd-sg-cormann-mcm-introductory-remarks-1-june-2021.htm.
72 Mathias Cormann, *Vision Statement for Secretary General of the Organisation for Economic Cooperation and Development*, https://www.cormannoecd.gov.au/sites/default/files/2020-11/vision_statement_eng_0.pdf.

3 Organization and functioning

This chapter provides an overview of the OECD's inner workings, its organizational structure, and decision-making procedures. To cope with membership enlargement and its burgeoning non-member relationships, since 2006 the Council has passed and implemented several resolutions pertaining the OECD's governance structure.[1] These declarations tweaked internal policymaking procedures but have not profoundly altered the roles and powers of the OECD's principal organs and offices. Thus, the functions of its bodies still derive from the articles of the OECD Convention and the Rules of Procedure of the Organisation, to which this chapter refers.[2] Whilst stipulating a generic framework, these documents accord OECD bodies leeway to fine-tune their modalities according to their needs and priorities. Unless the Council or Secretary-General decree otherwise, however, all OECD bodies sit in private (Rule 5), at the organization's Paris headquarters (Rule 4b), and proceed in English or French, the organization's two official languages (Rule 27).

Starting with the member states, this chapter introduces the central protagonists in the OECD drama and how their interactions propel the organization's agenda (see Figure 3.1). Although other factors intrude, the member states hold the reins and it is their interests and inputs that ultimately control the OECD's destiny. This is manifested in the OECD Council, the organization's executive chamber where members take collective decisions and direct its Programme of Work and Budget (PWB). The outcomes from the organization's "political" forums are filtered through more "administrative" structures that oversee the OECD's everyday activities. Headed by the Secretary-General, the secretariat provides the administrative, logistical, and analytical sinews to support the OECD's work. Albeit constrained by the member states, there is mounting evidence that the secretariat exerts a subtle, but significant, influence over the OECD's trajectory

DOI: 10.4324/9781351025867-4

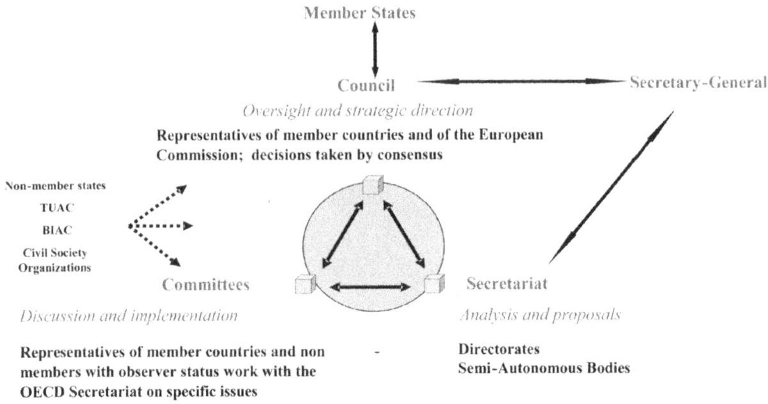

Figure 3.1 Who drives OECD work?
Source: Adapted from OECD, Organisation for Economic Cooperation and Development, available online at http://www.oecd.org/dataoecd/29/23/2397890.ppt (Accessed 7 August 2007).

(see Chapter 4).[3] The OECD committee system sits at the confluence of the political and administrative wings. The committees and their subsidiary bodies are the organization's "beating heart"[4] providing arteries of communication between OECD staff and member governments and chambers where national officials can gather to exchange information, contemplate the secretariat's analysis and review the implementation of best practices. The strategy of enlargement and outreach (see Chapters 2 and 6) has amplified the role of non-member states and civil society organizations in the OECD's work. The final part of the chapter slots these pieces of the OECD jigsaw together, showing how these actors work together to drive the organization's work, and concludes with a detailed exposition of the OECD peer review process.

Who drives OECD work?

Member States

The OECD's members are the single most important actors, determining the organization's substantive agenda in four principal ways. First, each member maintains a permanent delegation in Paris, which acts as the primary point of liaison between national capitals and the OECD Secretariat, and whose goal is to shape the organization's agenda to reflect their government's priorities. As well as representing their country on the OECD Council, the heads of national delegations also convene in informal settings, most notably as cabals of EU, APEC, Nordic, or G7/8 members, to share sentiments, float ideas, and prepare politically delicate decisions.[5] Second, officials from member governments overwhelmingly populate OECD committees often accompanied, in major bodies, by representatives of the permanent delegation. Third, through the Council, the members appoint and hold accountable the organization's executive head. Finally, OECD members supply most of the budget (Article 20.2), amounting to €398 million in 2021. The OECD's core (Part I) budget accounts for just over half of this funding. Beginning in 2008, a revised equation for budgetary contributions was gradually introduced whereby one third of the total is shared equally between members, with the residual calculated according to the country's economic weight and wealth (see Table 3.1). Supplementary (Part II) contributions account for another quarter of the budget and consist of funds voted by members and non-members to participate in non-core work programs. Salaries, pensions, and publications devour the remainder.

As a "one-member one-microphone organization,"[6] all OECD members are notionally equal, but economically powerful countries dominate. Despite reductions resulting from the adjusted formula, G7 states donated 55 percent of the Part I budget in 2019. These countries also maintain a stranglehold on key posts with almost half of OECD committee chairs and vice chairs hailing from the G7 (see Table 3.2). Only once in sixty years has the chair of the lynchpin EPC not been from the United Kingdom, the United States, Germany, or Japan. Similarly, while Article 11 empowers the Secretary-General to appoint secretariat staff based on merit and political interference is kept to a "workable minimum,"[7] powerful states wield considerable influence over senior appointments. Whereas larger states sustain dedicated and relatively bountiful missions to the OECD, teams from smaller countries sometimes combine their duties with diplomatic roles to other countries or international organizations.

One noteworthy anomaly is the quasi-membership of the European Commission. Having rejected its petition for full membership[8], Article 13 devolves the representation of the European Communities to Supplementary Protocol No.1 to the Convention. These arrangements give the European Commission the trappings of membership including a permanent delegation in Paris, a seat in the Council, the right to participate in OECD meetings (Rule 7a) and surveillance. Unlike ordinary members, the Commission does not contribute to the OECD budget and cannot vote when the Council is adopting legal acts.

Table 3.1 Scale of members' contributions to the OECD's core 'Part I' budget 2008 and 2019

Country	*Contribution 2008 (%)*	*Country*	*Contribution 2019 (%)*
United States	25.0	United States	20.5
Japan	16.0	Japan	9.4
Germany	9.1	Germany	7.2
United Kingdom	7.3	United Kingdom	5.4
France	6.7	France	5.2
Italy	5.5	Italy	4.0
Canada	3.6	Canada	3.5
Spain	3.6	South Korea	3.3
South Korea	2.4	Australia	3.1
Australia	2.1	Spain	3.0
Mexico	2.1	Mexico	2.7
Netherlands	2.1	Netherlands	2.2
Switzerland	1.5	Switzerland	2.2
Belgium	1.4	Turkey	2.2
Sweden	1.3	Belgium	1.7
Norway	1.2	Sweden	1.7
Austria	1.1	Norway	1.6
Denmark	1.0	Poland	1.6
Poland	1.0	Austria	1.5
Turkey	0.9	Israel	1.4
Greece	0.9	Denmark	1.4
Finland	0.8	Finland	1.3
Portugal	0.7	Ireland	1.3
Ireland	0.7	Chile	1.2
Czech Republic	0.5	Portugal	1.2
New Zealand	0.4	Czech Republic	1.1
Hungary	0.4	New Zealand	1.1
Slovak Republic	0.3	Greece	1.1
Luxembourg	0.2	Hungary	1.0
Iceland	0.2	Slovak Republic	1.0
		Slovenia	0.9
		Estonia	0.9
		Latvia	0.9
		Lithuania	0.9
		Luxembourg	0.8
		Iceland	0.6

Source: OECD, *Annual Report 2008* (Paris: OECD); OECD, "Member Countries' Budget Contributions for 2019," https://www.oecd.org/about/budget/member-countries-budget-contributions.htm.

Table 3.2 Chairs and Vice-Chairs of OECD committees and subsidiary bodies (June 2019)

Country	*Chairs*	*Vice-Chairs*	*Total*
United States	38	49	87
Japan	12	54	66
France	22	35	57
Canada	13	33	46
United Kingdom	16	30	46
Italy	13	22	35
Germany	12	20	32
Switzerland	16	14	30
Sweden	17	12	29
European Union	7	22	29
Netherlands	12	14	26
Norway	10	16	26
Belgium	12	14	26
Australia	10	13	23
South Korea	4	18	22
Finland	5	13	18
Spain	7	10	17
Austria	5	9	14
New Zealand	7	5	12
Portugal	4	8	12
Mexico	0	9	9
Turkey	2	6	8
Hungary	1	7	8
Slovenia	3	4	7
Chile	2	5	7
Denmark	2	4	6
Ireland	2	4	6
Poland	2	4	6
Israel	1	5	6
Czech Republic	2	3	5
Slovak Republic	3	1	4
Latvia	0	4	4
Luxembourg	1	2	3
Greece	0	3	3
Estonia	1	1	2
Iceland	1	0	1
Lithuania	0	1	1
Non-member states	14	23	37
International Organisations	1	0	1
Total	280	497	777

Source: OECD, "On-Line Guide to OECD Intergovernmental Activity," https://oecdgroups.oecd.org/.

Council

Under Article 7, the Council is composed of representatives from all member states and the European Commission and is the OECD's premier body "from which all acts of the Organization derive." The Council meets regularly at Permanent Representative level when it is attended by ambassadors and chaired by the Secretary-General (Article 10.2) and annually at Ministerial level (the MCM) where the attendees are ministerial portfolio holders from member states and a chair and two vice-chairs nominated by the Council preside (Article 8). Observers from the Business and Industry Advisory Committee (BIAC), the Trade Union Advisory Committee (TUAC), and other OECD social partners attend the annual meeting alongside those from multilateral economic organizations and, since 1999, selected non-members.

Theoretically, the Council exercises corresponding functions and powers irrespective of the level of the meeting. The Council imparts strategic control over the OECD by authorizing the Secretary-General to direct the secretariat to investigate certain subjects, evaluating their performance, adopting legal acts that bind signatories to varying degrees (Article 5, Rule 18), and making the final judgment about the accession of new members (Article 16). The Council also provides administrative oversight by creating and shuffling ancillary bodies to enable the OECD to accomplish its aims (Article 9), approving the budget (Article 20) and staff rules imposed by the Secretary-General (Article 11.1). Generally, however, meetings at Permanent Representative level tend to muse over routine matters, whereas MCMs are more strategically orientated and lend the OECD political impetus. The MCM is the pinnacle of the OECD cycle, whose communiqué recapitulates OECD norms and endorses priorities for the year ahead.

To improve its capacity to provide effective oversight and concentrate on strategic issues, the Council devolves operational issues to standing committees: the Audit, Budget, Executive, Evaluation, and External Relations Committees. Additionally, there have been slight changes to decision-making rules. Ordinarily the OECD takes decisions by consensus. Only in exceptional circumstances, and where members agree unanimously, do ballots occur on a one member, one vote basis. In these instances, the approval of a measure does not require unanimity, only that members abstain rather than vote against it. Resolutions then apply to all but the abstaining members. In July 2004, the OECD began experimenting with qualified majority voting (QMV) becoming permanent in 2006.[9] QMV can be applied in "special cases" where if a consensus cannot be attained a decision can be adopted provided it enjoys the support of 60 percent of members and is not opposed by three or more members who contribute a quarter of the Part I budget. Special cases include the approval or amendment of staff or financial regulations, the formation, perpetuation or disestablishment of committees and programs and, within limited parameters, the PWB. Nevertheless, most strategic decisions including accession, participation of non-members, adoption of the overall PWB, revisions to the organization's governance structures, and the passage or amendment of OECD Acts still require unanimity. In practice, QMV has been used sparingly, but the potential for its use has often encouraged a more constructive search for consensus.[10]

Secretary-General

As chair of the Council of Permanent Representatives (Article 10.2) and head of the secretariat, the Secretary-General is a critical valve linking national delegations with the OECD's everyday activities. In 2016, the rules governing the procedures for the selection of Secretaries-General were formalized.[11] Except for incumbents, an OECD member must propose candidates for the post of Secretary-General. A Selection Committee, drawn from the Heads of Delegation, facilitates the appointment process by arranging interviews with the nominees and conducting confidential conversations with permanent representatives. This process whittles down the field until a contender acceptable to all OECD members emerges. The Council then appoints the individual as Secretary-General for a five-year term (Article 10.1). While the Convention does not designate term limits, members now "consider that a Secretary-General should serve no more than two terms."[12]

The Secretary-General's power is constrained by the need to retain the member's support, but the vagaries of the OECD governance structure has allowed them all to leave their imprint (see Chapters 1 and 2). The Secretary-General determines the agenda of, and can make proposals to, any constituent body of the organization (Article 10, Rule 12). They decide how to discharge Council proclamations and orchestrate the secretariat to that end. The Secretary-General is also the external face of the organization, representing the OECD in national capitals and international institutions (Rule 24). The Secretary-General recommends to the Council the appointment of deputy secretaries-general to oversee discrete areas or initiatives.

Secretariat

The Secretariat exercises "all the functions necessary for the efficient administration of the Organization."[13] The Secretariat is subdivided into units and directorates that parallel and service the Council, the Office of the Secretary-General, the OECD's semi-autonomous bodies, and OECD committees (see Figure 3.2). Containing approximately 3,300 personnel recruited predominantly from member states, the OECD has the largest secretariat amongst international organizations outside the UN system. Of these staff, around one-third are economists, policy specialists, and other professionals that furnish the OECD committee system with administrative support, research, analysis, and proposals.

Whether and to what extent the bureaucracies of international organizations affect global governance is a vexed question. Traditionally, the OECD Secretariat is sketched as a regiment which, in the words of former Secretary-General Angel Gurria, gets its "marching orders and......we produce the piece of research that was asked of us."[14] Rather

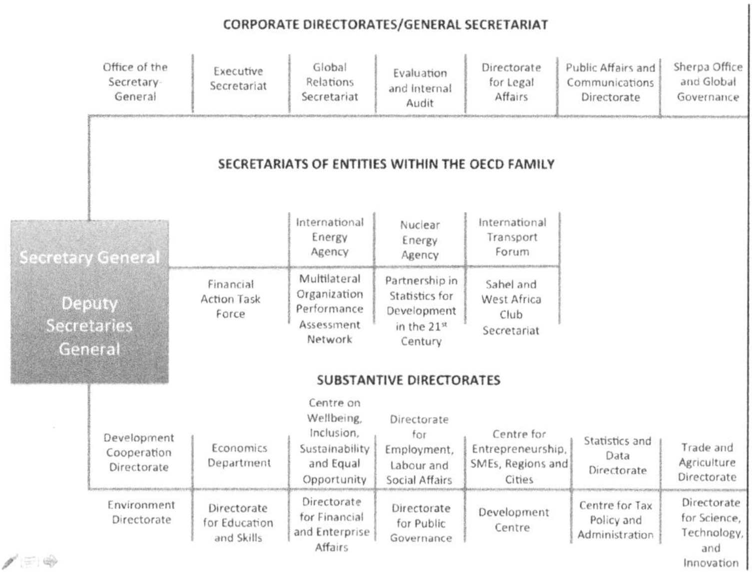

Figure 3.2 OECD organization chart
Source: OECD, *OECD Secretary-General's Report to Ministers 2021* (Paris: OECD, 2021), 28-9.

than mere *automatons* passively serving the members, other seasoned OECD practitioners claim that the secretariat exhibits considerable *autonomy* and that "new initiatives seldom come from national delegations" but "an innovative international secretariat."[15] Certainly there are examples, including the bringing of education into the organization's purview[16] and the "problems of modern society" (see Chapter 1), where the entrepreneurialism of the secretariat was instrumental in reshaping the OECD's substantive agenda. By framing an issue in a particular way, it is possible for the secretariat to convince states of the existence of a problem, that it is in their national interest to resolve it, and that the OECD is the most logical venue for this purpose. For the most part, however, the secretariat's influence is more elusive and subsequent to the members instructing the OECD to interrogate an issue. As one retired senior OECD official observes, the submissions of the secretariat "are prepared from an independent and transnational point of view, it is the clients—the member governments—that *largely* determine the choice, and *up to a point the treatment*, of the subject matter (my emphasis)."[17] In other words, the secretariat has some liberty to interpret the member's edicts. The secretariat's margin for maneuver is accentuated by the choice of the OECD to address virgin terrains. In these circumstances, it falls to the Secretariat to interpret the nature of the problem, the questions that will be asked, and elaborate the vocabulary to describe it. The detailed technical knowledge possessed by the secretariat allows it to craft the optics through which the gaze of its political masters are refracted. For instance, the OECD's work on "trade in services" (see Chapter 1) arose spontaneously from the inquiries of the secretariat following the member's more general request to anticipate emergent trade issues.[18]

In this way, the OECD's agenda emerges iteratively via a "tango, danced by the Ministerial Council and the Secretariat."[19] Nevertheless, the influence of the secretariat should not be exaggerated. Needing to retain the support of those holding the purse strings, the secretariat operates with "one hand behind their back."[20] The secretariat can exert a significant impact on the OECD agenda but countries regularly block research likely to produce conclusions they do not want to hear.[21] Recently, the obsession with measuring results, combined with the growing proportion of OECD staff on shorter-term and project specific contracts or seconded from national governments, has tightened the constraints on the secretariat's independence.[22] In the end, the secretariat's autonomy is conditional on it producing work that is relevant to, and respects the sentiments of, the members.

Committees

In practice, the Council delegates many of the powers vested in it by the OECD Convention to a warren of committees that it instructs to study specific questions (Rule 22a). The committees are responsible for the OECD's principal outputs, the policy prescriptions, blueprints, and best practices which, albeit infrequently and pending Council certification, can be the basis for soft law instruments. As custodians of the organization's peer reviews processes (see Box 3.1), committees are also responsible for monitoring the enactment of OECD instruments.

Within bounds set by the Council,[23] committees may delve into any question within their competence (Rule 22b) and customize their working routines and relationships with non-members. Consequently, committees are versatile mechanisms that have developed differing traits according to the nature of the policy arena they oversee. What follows is therefore a general overview of their composition, structure and functions. Intermittently, OECD committees meet in ministerial session to launch, provide impetus to, or conclude a major project but normally are chiefly populated by envoys from permanent delegations and national capitals. Every year over 40,000 delegates attend meetings at the OECD. Indeed, the level of engagement by national delegates is a key distinguishing feature of OECD committees when compared with their equivalents in other international economic organizations. This has several important implications. First, it results in a symbiotic relationship between the secretariat and their clients (national government departments). Most top-level committees congregate only once or twice per year, but the need to prepare future meetings and the more frequent sittings of their subsidiary groups (see below), necessitate open channels of communication between the secretariat and national capitals. This process allows national governments to steer the secretariat's work and the OECD staff to anticipate the likely responses of their clients in the search for consensus.[24] Second, the presence of high-ranking government officials enables ideas gleaned at the OECD to be relayed back into national policymaking, especially as they are conscious that their record for doing so is subject to monitoring and peer review (see Box 3.1). Third, by repeatedly bringing together government officials to exchange information and experiences on shared challenges OECD committees fuse the participants into "global knowledge networks"[25] possessing authoritative expertise which they exploit to orient the global policymaking agenda (see Chapter 4).

Each committee has a bureau, consisting of an elected chair (authorized by the Council) and vice-chairs chosen by the committee,

Table 3.3 OECD committees by directorate (July 2019)

Directorate	*Main Committees*	*Subgroups*	*Total*
Centre for Entrepreneurship, SMEs, Regions and Cities	3	2	5
Centre for Tax Policy and Administration	3	20	23
Development Co-operation Directorate	1	7	8
Directorate for Education and Skills	4	12	16
Directorate for Employment, Labour and Social Affairs	2	8	10
Directorate for Financial and Enterprise Affairs	6	20	26
Directorate for Science, Technology and Innovation	6	12	18
Economics Department	2	5	7
Environment Directorate	2	23	25
General Secretariat	1	12	13
International Energy Agency	1	14	15
Inter-organization Study Section on Salaries and Prices	1	2	3
OECD Nuclear Energy Agency	1	77	78
Public Governance Directorate	2	16	18
Sahel and West Africa Club	0	1	1
Statistics and Data Directorate	1	4	5
Trade and Agriculture Directorate	4	20	24
Total	**40**	**255**	**295**

Source: OECD, "On-Line Guide to OECD Intergovernmental Activity," https://oecdgroups.oecd.org/.

to guide its business. A secretary, normally a senior secretariat official, assists them. To facilitate their work, committees may establish subsidiary bodies (Rule 21b) to grapple with specific or nettlesome problems. Today, there are just shy of 300 OECD committees, working parties, and expert groups (see Table 3.3). Most of these bodies entitle all OECD and selected non-OECD countries to membership.

Non-members and civil society

Under the auspices of its global relations strategy, the OECD is taking steps to consolidate and diversify relations with non-members and civil society organizations (see Chapters 2 and 6). Article 12 states that "upon such terms and conditions as the Council may determine" the OECD may ".......invite non-member Governments or organisations to participate in the activities of the Organisation." The OECD does not confer organization-wide observer status preferring instead a stratified system that permits individual subsidiary bodies to calibrate the extensity and intensity of non-member, or "partners" in OECD parlance, involvement. The lowest tier is "Invitees," consisting of non-members that are invited to participate in, and contribute to, individual meetings. Invitees may be barred from part of the meeting (Rule 9b) may only report to the meeting with the chair's assent (Rule 9c) and are neither embroiled in nor bound by the body's decisions. The intermediate tier is "Participants" that, subject to a biennial review, are invited to attend all meetings of a subsidiary body on a continuing basis. Participants are expected to "contribute substantially to the body's mandate and programme of work"[26] by intervening in discussions, proposing agenda items and providing information. Participants may express a preference to be bound by the body's decisions. The highest tier is "Associates" who may participate in the entirety of the body's activities, including its decision making and peer review processes and its bureau. Associates are expected to demonstrate commitment to the body's goals through their policies and adherence to its most important codes and standards as decided by the committee in charge.

This graduated approach, together with the latitude of committees to govern their interactions with external parties, produces a kaleidoscope of relationships between the OECD and non-member states. Over the last decade, there has been a significant uptick in non-member state incorporation in OECD work. For example, instances of non-members adhering to OECD legal instruments and being invited to participate in OECD bodies have almost trebled since 2010 (see Figures 3.3 and 3.4). In October 2020, 77 non-member countries were partners of one or more subsidiary body but 19 countries, the OECD's Key Partners, G20 states, prospective members, and Country Programme participants, account for 70 percent of those relationships. This bias is even more pronounced among Participants and Associates where these countries account for 80 percent of current invitations (see Table 3.4). These countries are likewise responsible for 63 per cent of the adherences to OECD legal instruments.[27] Beyond this, approximately fifty international organizations regularly participate in OECD work, led by the Bretton Woods institutions, the UN's semi-autonomous and specialized agencies, regional multilateral development banks and a panoply of institutions associated with European regional integration.

The conditions for civil society enmeshment are fleshed out in a 1962 Council decision[28] which gives the OECD considerable discretion to

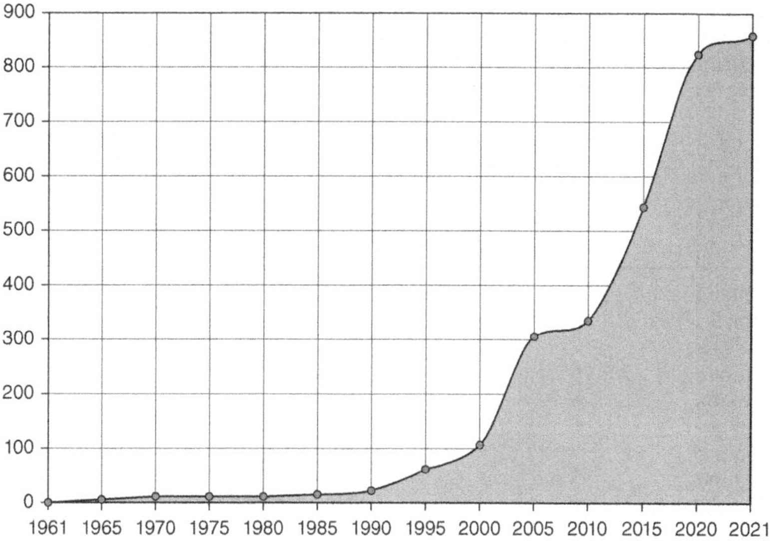

Figure 3.3 Number of non-member adherences to OECD legal instruments
Source: OECD, *OECD Legal Instruments: Key Figures*, https://legalinstruments.oecd.org/en/stats.

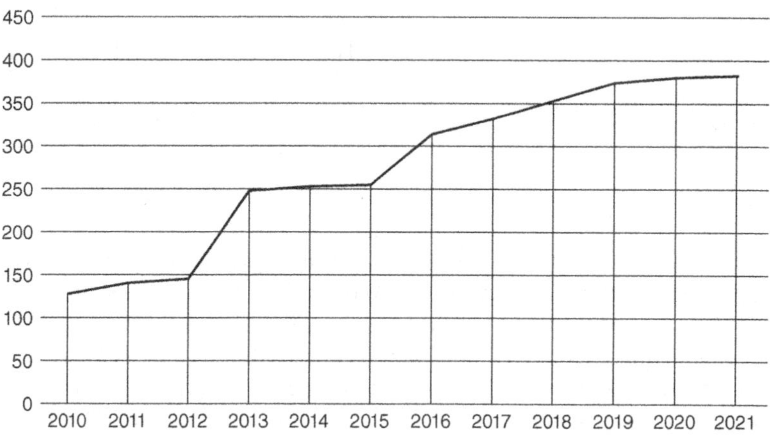

Figure 3.4 Invitations to non-members to participate in OECD bodies as participant or associate
Source: *The Secretary-General's Report to Ministers on Global Relations: OECD Global Relations: Serving the OECD and its Members with global impact*, C/MIN(2021)8, 10.

Table 3.4 Key partners, G20 countries, prospective members and other selected partners: Involvement in OECD bodies, projects, programs, legal instruments

	Number of Partnerships in Bodies and Projects			*Number of OECD Legal Instruments*		
	As Associate/ Member	*As Participant*	*Total*	*Adherence Confirmed*	*Adherence Requested*	*Total*
Argentina	12	17	**29**	51	6	**57**
Brazil	14	23	**37**	99	45	**144**
Bulgaria	7	5	**12**	32	6	**38**
China	6	5	**11**	9	0	**9**
Croatia	8	4	**12**	26	5	**31**
Egypt	6	6	**12**	21	1	**22**
India	7	9	**16**	14	0	**14**
Indonesia	5	5	**10**	15	0	**15**
Kazakhstan	8	13	**21**	39	5	**44**
Morocco	9	2	**11**	30	3	**33**
Peru	7	11	**18**	45	2	**47**
Romania	14	8	**22**	50	4	**54**
Russian Federation	7	22	**29**	27	0	**27**
Saudi Arabia	2	5	**7**	7	0	**7**
South Africa	6	20	**26**	23	1	**24**
Thailand	5	4	**9**	7	0	**7**
Tunisia	7	1	**8**	21	0	**21**
Ukraine	7	4	**11**	23	1	**24**
Vietnam	3	1	**4**	6	0	**6**

Source: OECD, *The Secretary-General's Report to Ministers on Global Relations: OECD Global Relations: Serving the OECD and its Members with global impact*, C/MIN(2021)8, 8.

consult with almost any non-governmental organization. The OECD's most prominent and persistent civil society associations are with TUAC, "an interface for trade unions with the OECD,"[29] and BIAC, "an officially recognized business voice to the OECD."[30] Officially, TUAC and BIAC do not possess a privileged position needing, like all civil society groups, to negotiate access to relevant OECD bodies. That said, uniquely among civil society partners, TUAC and BIAC are invited to the MCM and its preparatory meetings and maintain permanent, albeit tiny, secretariats in Paris. The BIAC and TUAC secretariats also have superior access to OECD documents.[31] Despite their propinquity to the OECD, resource limitations mean BIAC and TUAC attend few substantive meetings.

Since the 1990s, the OECD's interface with civil society has undergone significant transformation (see Chapter 2). Based historically on a largely one-way communication of information, the OECD has recently placed greater emphasis on dialogue with, and the participation of, civil society organizations in its work.[32] The avenues for civil society consultation with the OECD have multiplied and a dedicated Public Affairs and Communications (PAC) Directorate provides an overarching framework to nurture and govern these relationships.

The OECD's appetite for civil society engagement has produced some notable innovations, not least the Annual Forum. The Annual Forum is a "multistakeholder summit,"[33] which brings business and political leaders together with those from civil society, trade unions, academia, and the media. Held immediately prior to the MCM and aligned around a chosen theme, the Forum has attracted over 25,000 delegates since its inception in 2000. Nevertheless, committees continue to be the main conduit for civil society input into the OECD. As with non-members, committees may attune their relationship with civil society organizations. The requirement that a committee's choice of civil society interlocutors needs the Secretary-General's approval (Rule 10b) is today delegated to the responsible OECD Directorate. Some committees have longstanding and widespread civil society connections. For instance, 7,000 representatives from industry, academia, trade unions, and environmental groups convene in the working groups of the Environment Committee to renew and police the Good Laboratory Practices that underpin the OECD's Mutual Acceptance of Data in the Assessment of Chemicals.[34] Others are of a more recent vintage, but have stimulated important developments including rearing alliances of non-governmental organizations that have become important OECD intermediaries. The consultation that led to the OECD's Guidelines for Multinational Enterprises, for example, strengthened the bonds between groups looking to promote corporate accountability and sustainable investment. This inspired OECDWatch, now a 130 strong network of organizations, that monitors the implementation and effectiveness of these guidelines and carried out their update in 2011. Elsewhere committees are making greater use of online platforms to solicit the opinions of civil society groups. Reflecting their importance to the delivery of development initiatives, the DAC is another OECD body whose links with CSOs are extensive and increasingly institutionalized.

Compared with 20 years ago, the OECD now has "a more heterogeneous set of civil society actors regularly assuming more substantial roles across a wider range of policy areas."[35] Scratch the veneer, however, and the changes are not as startling as they first appear. The OECD still errs on the side of caution in its civil society relationships, tending to indulge corporate and commercial interests that are sympathetic to its philosophy at the expense of those wishing to curb market arbitration of human activity.[36] Avoiding a throng of competing viewpoints allows the OECD to preserve its decision-making capacity (a condition of the 1962 decision) but possibly at the expense of the legitimacy of those processes and their outputs.[37] Additionally, the accommodation of civil society is highly uneven across the organization. While areas such as trade, development, agriculture, environment, and fiscal affairs have respectable linkages with civil society, the economic committees, the bellwethers of OECD policies, remain aloof.

Putting it all together: The OECD's way of working

Reflecting the license given to subsidiary bodies, there is inevitably some variation in working practices across the organization. Nevertheless, it is possible to discern a distinctive "OECD way" of working (see Figure 3.5). Once a decision is taken at the Council to study a policy problem at the OECD, the next step is for the secretariat to collect the requisite data. Recall that Article 3(a) obliges members

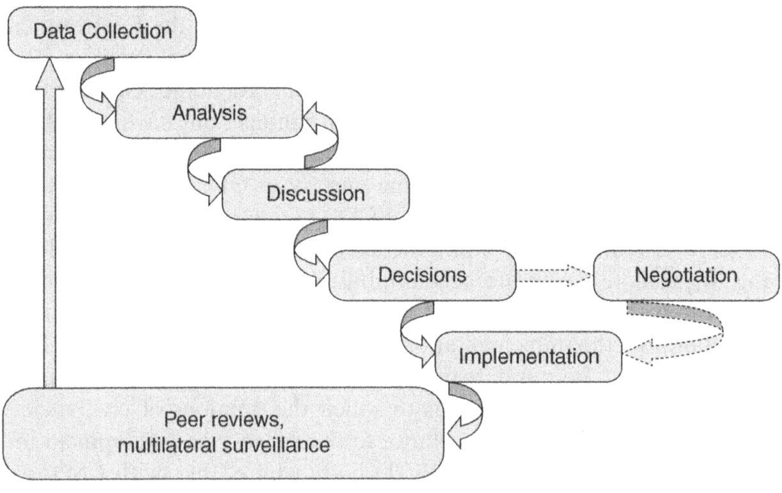

Figure 3.5 The OECD's way of working
Source: adapted from OECD, *Organisation for Economic Cooperation and Development* (Paris: OECD, 2007).

to supply the organization "with the information necessary for the accomplishment of its tasks," a provision extended to non-members where they are Associate partners in OECD activities. Information takes a variety of forms, from regularized statistical returns to more abstract qualitative data detailing the experiences, ideas, and opinions of national policymakers. When the OECD secretariat wrestles with new problems, it is frequently necessary for them to determine the data that needs to be collected. This might involve pioneering techniques to reconcile and render comparable competing national yardsticks but can also entail working from scratch to define, conceive terminology to describe, and invent standardized indicators and methodologies to measure, social and economic phenomena.

Guided by the subsidiary bodies and national delegations, stage two sees the secretariat sift and process the data to identify trends, correlations, and causations, test hypothesis, zoom in on areas of consensus and controversy, diagnose problems, and lay out a range of possible solutions. In the third phase of the OECD work cycle, these findings are exposed to political realities through discussion in the OECD's committees and working groups. Using the secretariat's commentary and analysis as a point of departure, participants congregate in the OECD's subsidiary bodies to formally explicate national positions. This is an iterative process often requiring additional research and analysis by the secretariat to propel the debate. Through these discussions, the participants learn about the policy experiences of their counterparts and gradually come to view problems through common conceptual and analytical lenses. In this way, it becomes possible for states to identify or refine their interests in relation to the problem and move to the fourth stage of the policy cycle involving convergence around acceptable solutions or standards.

Sporadically, countries take these decisions one stage further using the consensus reached as a springboard to negotiate a legally codified instrument for adoption in the Council. In total, 461 substantive legal instruments have been agreed within the framework of the OEEC and OECD, of which 251 remain in force as of November 2021.[38] The most formal of these are 24 OECD Decisions that, unless they abstain when it is adopted, "shall be binding on all the Members."[39] Strictly speaking, OECD Decisions are not international treaties but "they do entail, for Member countries, the same kind of legal obligations."[40] Most OECD Acts take the form of Recommendations "submitted to the Members for consideration in order that they may, if they consider it opportune, provide for their implementation."[41] The 173 Recommendations active in November 2021 "are not legally binding, but practice accords them great moral force as representing the political will of the Member countries."[42] Ergo, OECD instruments overwhelming take the form of "soft" law whose texts are non-binding but nevertheless embody norms or preferences about expected standards of future behavior.

Whatever their legal standing, the expectation is that states making commitments at the OECD will do their utmost to implement them. As Chapter 4 discusses, the incentive to do so arises not from the looming threat of material sanctions but peer pressure arising from shared expectations about appropriate behavior. Multilateral surveillance is the cornerstone of the OECD way, the most formalized aspect of which are its peer review processes. As the name suggests, peer reviews comprise forensic evaluations of a country's performance in a specific arena by other countries party to an OECD body or agreement. Peer reviews gauge the extent to which states comply with OECD best practices, and, where frailties are found, exhort them to reform. Beyond their monitoring role, peer reviews help to close the OECD policy loop yielding new data and insights about strategies that work, stimulating fresh analysis and discussion and laying the foundations for future guidelines and standards.

While there is some variation between the peer review processes of different committees, all follow a common structural and procedural template. Structurally, every peer review process has a protocol enumerating the benchmarks against which a country's record will be measured, the agents responsible for the review, procedures for finalizing the outcome, and the frequency with which it occurs. Most peer reviews are concerted efforts between officials from the secretariat, the country under review, and other countries in the OECD body. Typically, the secretariat pilots the preliminary phases of the review alongside a couple of "lead" countries designated by the relevant committee. All members are then involved in the final phase. In these latter stages, peer reviews have customs for fashioning and disseminating the results. The length of the peer review cycle fluctuates. Peer reviews of economic policies and the Economic Surveys (see Box 3.1) occur biennially, whereas those of environmental policies happen every eight to ten years.

Procedurally, peer reviews have three phases. Phase one is preparatory and involves the secretariat gathering background data and the country under review assessing its own performance. Phase two is consultative. Here a team from the secretariat and the countries leading the review are immersed in a thoroughgoing dialogue and on-site visits with the state whose performance is under the microscope. The review team prepares a draft report for consideration in the last phase of the process, the assessment. The assessment summons a delegation from the state under review before a plenary session of the applicable OECD body for

BOX 3.1

OECD *ECONOMIC SURVEYS*

The *Economic Surveys* are among the most cited OECD outputs. They merit special attention because they represent the culmination of the oldest OECD peer review process since emulated by other Directorates. The OECD supervises Economic Surveys through the Economics Department (ECO) and, more specifically, the Economic and Development Review Committee (EDRC). The Economic Survey aims to provide insights into the policy challenges and economic standing of individual countries, enhance national and international economic policy debates, evaluate each country's performance against OECD macroeconomic and structural policy yardsticks, and recommend therapies to deliver sustainable long-term economic growth.

The preparatory phase of the Economic Survey sees a country desk in ECO amass background information about the country under review. National officials submit a memorandum covering recent economic developments and projections. To solicit further information and refine the verdicts in the questionnaire, an ECO delegation visits and rendezvous with senior members of the central bank, economic ministries plus a variety of experts and social partners in the country concerned. The findings provide the material for a draft report by the Secretariat, marking the start of the review's consultative phase. Interested parties peruse the draft and the country under review prepares a rejoinder ahead of a follow-up visit from ECO staff. This expedition enables the Secretariat to renew the original data and trigger discussions on fallibilities diagnosed in the draft Survey. This consultative phase ends with a convocation of OECD staff and senior officials (and sometimes Ministers) before the ECO outfit withdraws to Paris to compile the final draft Survey.

The assessment phase of the process embarks with the circulation of the draft Survey and, about four weeks later, a plenary session of the EDRC where a delegation from the country under review is grilled by their peers. The themes to be broached and the bearings of the discussion are primed by a "Questions for Discussion Note" jointly contrived by the Secretariat and officials from the two countries handpicked by the EDRC as lead reviewers. The meeting commences with testimony by the country under review where it can rehearse points of dispute with the draft survey and justify policy choices. Delegates from lead review countries then lead a cross-examination. Once the discussion has run its course, the chair summarizes the meeting and stresses revisions for inclusion in the final survey. The following day the team from the country under review thrashes out with the Secretariat a version of the document that they are happy to see published. Generally, revisions are minor and involve expunging politically sensitive advice. This is because the report must be approved unanimously and members are unlikely to brook a report that ignores their collective advice. Once the report is approved, it is published under EDRC auspices and made available to the public.

Sources: Fabrizio Pagani, *Peer Review: A Tool for Co-operation and Change: An Analysis of an OECD Working Method* (Paris: OECD, 2002), 22–24; Armin Schafer, "A new form of governance? Comparing the open method of co-ordination to multilateral surveillance by the IMF and the OECD," *Journal of European Public Policy* 13, no. 1 (2006): 73–75; Maria Duclos Lindstrom, "The dual messages of OECD economic surveys: Observations from the OECD's Economics Department and the drafting and peer review of Economic Surveys," *Economic Sociology* 19, no. 2 (2018): 19–24.

an inquisition about the draft report. Following these discussions, participants hammer out an agreed document for public consumption.

Conclusion

This chapter has sketched the nuts and bolts of the OECD, introducing the role and function of the organization's constituent parts and how they work together with states, and increasingly a myriad of non-members, to spur its agenda. Several key themes from this chapter reverberate through the rest of the book. First, states, especially the member countries, pilot the OECD. Their sway over the organization is exerted via the power of the purse, the choice of Secretary-General, and representation in committees where their delegates far outnumber those from the OECD secretariat. The member governments decide what the OECD should be working on, but it is possible for the organization's staff to nudge the agenda and how particular problems are contemplated. Chapter 4 itemizes the various ways this activity affects the course of global governance. Second, the chapter hints at the scale and scope of OECD activity covered further in Chapter 5. Serving across 13 policy directorates and eight special bodies, the OECD's almost 300 strong system of committees and working groups delve into almost every social and economic issue of relevance to its clients in national governments. Finally, there is an inkling of the growing weight of non-member countries and non-state actors at the OECD which, as Chapter 6 suggests, is calling into question the sustainability of the organization's working methods and governance structure.

Notes

1 OECD, *Resolutions of the Council on the Governance of the Organisation*, C(2015)100.
2 OECD, *Rules of Procedure of the Organisation* (Paris: OECD, 2013).
3 See, for example, Jan Enkler, Sylvia Schmidt, Steffen Eckhard, Christoph Knill and Stephan Grohs, "Administrative Styles in the OECD: Bureaucratic Policy-Making beyond Formal Rules," *International Journal of Public Administration* 40, no. 8 (2017): 637–48.
4 Peter Carroll and Aynsley Kellow, *The OECD: A Study of Organizational Adaptation* (Cheltenham: Edward Elgar, 2011), 18.
5 OECD, *Resolutions of the Council on the Governance of the Organisation*, C(2015)100, 4.
6 A depiction of the OECD gleaned in an informal conversation with Richard Carey, former Director of the Development Cooperation Directorate.

7 Angel Gurria, "The OECD at 50: Past Achievements, Present Challenges and Future Directions," *Global Policy* 2, no. 3 (2011): 319.
8 Carroll and Kellow, *The OECD: A Study of Organizational Adaptation*, 202–3.
9 OECD, *Resolution of the Council on a New Governance Structure for the Organisation*, C(2006)78/FINAL.
10 Jocelyne Bourgon, "Reform and Modernization of the OECD," *Centre for International Governance Innovation Working Paper* No. 42 (2009), 13–15.
11 OECD, *Resolution of the Council on the Procedure for Appointing Future Secretaries-General*, C(2016)70/FINAL.
12 Ibid., 2.
13 OECD, *OECD: History, Aims, Structure* (Paris: OECD, 1971), 35.
14 Quoted in Leslie Pal, *Frontiers of Governance: The OECD and Global Public Management* (Basingstoke: Palgrave, 2012), 2.
15 Alexander King, *Let the Cat Turn Around: One Man's Traverse of the Twentieth Century* (London: CPTM, 2007), 276.
16 See George S. Papadopoulos, *Education 1960–1990: The OECD Perspective* (Paris: OECD, 1994), 37–41.
17 David Henderson, "The Role of the OECD in Liberalising International Trade and Capital Flows," *The World Economy* 19, no. 5 (1996): 14 (my emphasis).
18 Geza Feketekuty, *International Trade in Services: An Overview and Blueprint for Negotiations* (Cambridge, M.A.: Ballinger, 1988).
19 Pal, *Frontiers of Governance: The OECD and Global Public Management*, 2.
20 Martin Marcussen and Jarle Trondal, "The OECD Civil Servant: Caught between Scylla and Charybdis," *Review of International Political Economy* 18, no. 5 (2011): 611.
21 See for example, Robert Wolfe, "The OECD Contribution to the Evolution of Twenty-First Century Trade Law," *George Washington International Law Review* 43, no. 2 (2011): 291.
22 Judith Clifton and Daniel Diaz-Fuentes, "From 'Club of the Rich' to 'Globalisation a la carte?' Evaluating Reform at the OECD," *Global Policy* 2, no. 3 (2011): 305.
23 OECD, *Deepening Enhanced Engagement: Guidelines to Committees*, C(2010)100/Final.
24 On this see Carroll and Kellow, *The OECD: A Study of Organisational Adaptation*, 17–22; Peter Carroll and Aynsley Kellow, *Middle Powers and International Organisations* (Cheltenham: Edward Elgar, 2017), 16–19; David Henderson, "International Economic Cooperation Revisited," *Government and Opposition* 28, no. 1 (1993): 18–24.
25 Tony Porter and Michael Webb, "Role of the OECD in the Orchestration of Global Knowledge Networks," in *The OECD and Transnational Governance*, eds. Rianne Mahon and Stephen McBride (Vancouver: UBC Press, 2008), 43–59.
26 OECD, *Revised Resolution of the Council on Partnerships in OECD Bodies*, C(2012)100/REV1/FINAL, 3.
27 OECD, *The Secretary-General's Report to Ministers on Global Relations: OECD Global Relations: Serving the OECD and its Members with global impact*, C/MIN(2021)8, 7.

28 OECD, *Decision of the Council on Relations with International Non-Governmental Organizations*, OECD C(62)45(1962).
29 TUAC, "Home," tuac.org.
30 BIAC, "Business at OECD," https://biac.org/quick-facts/.
31 OECD, *Audit of the Consultation with Civil Society by the OECD*, C(2018)94/PART2/ADD2/VOL1/FINAL, 6.
32 John West, "The Emergence of Multi-stakeholder Diplomacy at the OECD: Origins, Lessons and Directions for the Future," Paper presented to the International Conference on Multi-Stakeholder Diplomacy, Malta, 11–13 February 2005, 7–11; OECD, *OECD's co-operative activities with civil society*, C/INF(2010)1.
33 John West, "The Emergence of Multi-stakeholder Diplomacy at the OECD: Origins, Lessons and Directions for the Future," 10.
34 James Salzman, "Decentralized Administrative Law in the Organization for Economic Cooperation and Development," *Law and Contemporary Problems* 68, no. 3–4 (2005): 200–03.
35 Richard Woodward, "Towards Complex Multilateralism? Civil Society and the OECD," in *The OECD and Transnational Governance*, eds. Rianne Mahon and Stephen McBride (Vancouver: UBC Press, 2008), 91.
36 Ibid., 87–94; OECD, *Audit of the Consultation with Civil Society by the OECD*, 7.
37 OECD, *Progress Report on Standard-Setting Review*, C/MIN(2019)13, 17.
38 OECD, "OECD Legal Instruments," https://legalinstruments.oecd.org/en/?_gl=1*1vz61sy*_ga*MzE5OTU1OTcwLjE2MzgyNjczMjM.*_ga_F7KSNTXTRX*MTYzODQ0NzY5OS4zLjAuMTYzODQ0NzY5OS4w.
39 OECD, "Convention on the Organisation for Economic Cooperation and Development," https://www.oecd.org/general/conventionontheorganisationforeconomicco-operationanddevelopment.htm.
40 Nicola Bonucci, "The Legal Status of an OECD Act and the Procedure for Its Adoption," https://www.oecd.org/education/skills-beyond-school/31691605.pdf.
41 OECD, *Rules of Procedure of the Organization*, 12.
42 Nicola Bonucci, "The Legal Status of an OECD Act and the Procedure for Its Adoption."

4 The OECD and global governance

Weathervane or weather maker?

This chapter assesses how and why the OECD's activities influence global governance. A trawl through the websites of most OECD governments quickly reveals dozens, if not hundreds, of references to the OECD and its outputs. The OECD's data, reports, and benchmarks are widely cited by journalists, parliamentarians, and CSOs to substantiate or discredit policy proposals or performance. Beyond the OECD, the organization's statistics, concepts, and standards influence debates in an increasing number of non-member states and, as is it has throughout, support the ongoing circus of international summitry (see also Chapter 6). Official pronouncements by OECD personnel are frequently couched in terms of the impact of the organization's work on national policies, crisis management, or global attitudes to contemporary problems. As Emile van Lennep put it, "the formulation of economic policies, with the clear intention that our objective is to make our impact on governments, is the heart of the matter at the OECD."[1] Most academic literature likewise acknowledges that, despite eschewing the limelight, the OECD has exerted a "subtle discipline"[2] over global policy making.

While there is almost universal agreement that the OECD influences global governance, the extent of that influence and the mechanisms through which it arises are matters of empirical and theoretical dispute. Empirically many studies have established correlations between OECD recommendations and national policies but concede that it is tricky to disentangle the OECD's imprint from those of other institutions of global governance.[3] The nature and scope of the OECD's influence is also interpreted very differently according to the theoretical lenses through which the organization is viewed. Having long been dominated by approaches whose assumptions largely reduced the OECD to a bystander in global governance, contemporary scholarship suggests that the organization actively configures the global agenda and the type of world that is to be governed.

DOI: 10.4324/9781351025867-5

Considerations of the OECD's role in global governance share several similarities. First, they agree about the OECD's way of working and the functions it performs, namely as a reservoir of authoritative data and policy analysis, a forum for deliberation on matters of mutual concern and the evolution of rules, norms and principles to govern them, and a monitor and evaluator of economic trends both nationally and globally (see Figure 3.5). Second, they recognize that member interests and the underlying power structures of the global economy arbitrate the extent of OECD influence. Finally, given the paltry legal and financial instruments at its disposal, they concur that knowledge and ideas are the main currencies in which the OECD deals.[4] Where their views deviate, however, is in understanding how and why the OECD's knowledge and ideas shape global governance.

Underpinned by rationalist accounts of international organizations, one version holds that the OECD's activities have little independent impact on global governance. In an increasingly interdependent world, states recognize that securing their interests requires international cooperation. Unfortunately, the prospects for international cooperation are plagued by uncertainty about the causes of governance problems and prospective solutions, the preferences of counterparties, and their willingness to abide by agreements. The knowledge and ideas excavated by the OECD and shared in its committees, plus the organization's routine surveillance practices, supplies the information states need to overcome these uncertainties and evolve norms or bargain about rules to govern collective problems. States agree and comply with these norms and rules when it is in their interests to do so, based on a rational calculation of costs and benefits. The OECD is thus pictured as a neutral venue in which states pursue predetermined interests. Outcomes at the OECD are largely mediated by prevailing patterns of material power from which the interests of states derive. The rationalist account presents the OECD as nothing more than an environment that allows states to realize their interests more efficiently than bilateral partnerships or an accomplice of US hegemony providing a veneer of legitimacy to America's leadership of the global economy.[5] The OECD is, in short, a weathervane.

Conversely, a second interpretation, informed by constructivist approaches to international organization, suggests the OECD is a weather maker whose work generates breezes (and occasional gales) that alter the bearing of global governance. Far from being just a forum for interstate bargaining based on pre-existing interests, the OECD is a place where states learn about the world and the interests they have. Unlike the rationalists, who privilege material explanations, the constructivists foreground the role of ideas and knowledge in understanding what makes global governance hang together. Although not oblivious to material forces, this perspective contends that the interests and identities of states, plus the standards of behavior to which they aspire, arise in part through encountering new ideas. The OECD's significance to global governance lies its aptitude for generating and disseminating authoritative ideas and knowledge about the world and offering opportunities for actors to discuss them.

Residing in the secretariat and the specialists from national capitals, international organizations, and civil society that attend its meetings, the authority of OECD ideas and outputs rests on the expertise of these appointees. Their possession of superior technical competence confers upon them the ability to frame problems and delimit the realm of acceptable and feasible policy responses that, over time, states are socialized into accepting as norms that guide their behavior. Importantly, it is recognized that some of the ideas emanating from the OECD originate with the secretariat rather than the members. Consequently, the OECD can nudge the global governance agenda by spotlighting priority issues and educating countries about their interest in addressing them and the best means of doing so. Furthermore, norms circulating at the OECD also contribute to the individual and collective identity of the members, in turn altering expectations about the role they ought to play and appropriate standards of behavior. States align their behavior with OECD norms because, as the self-professed club of "leading," "advanced," or "modern" states, they represent the gold standard for countries who regard themselves as belonging to that community.

OECD 1.0—A weathervane in global governance

From the prevention of economic instability and the spread of infectious disease to the mitigation of climate change and tax avoidance, the process of globalization continues to place a daunting list of problems beyond the capacity of states to govern in isolation. In these circumstances, it seems axiomatic that states should cooperate to attain their shared interests in tackling these predicaments, but imperfect information makes it difficult for rational actors to decide if cooperation is worthwhile. Holding an instrumental view of the OECD, the rationalists believe that it enhances international policymaking by supplying an institutional apparatus through which states, led by the most powerful, can obtain the knowledge they need to start and sustain episodes of cooperation.

Production of information and knowledge, in different forms, is intrinsic to all phases in the OECD's way of working (see Figure 3.5). Chapter 3 noted that Article 3(a) of the convention establishes a basis for the routine collection by the OECD of data from participating states. The OECD secretariat maneuver this data to provide internationally comparable statistics often contriving new or composite indicators to quantify emergent concepts, benchmark progress against international norms or estimate the likely payoffs from policy choices. Owing largely to the quality of its statistical processes, participants regard the OECD's data and the analyses that flow from it as authoritative and independent.[6] As such, they are respected as a trustworthy foundation on which discussions about an issue might proceed. For example, during the 1960s, an absence of uniform balance of payments statistics allowed states to nullify criticisms in WP3 by rehearsing justifications of their approach by reference to domestically produced numbers and forecasts. The OECD's evolution of a common metric to refine the speed, completeness, and comparability of the data "marked the transition to franker discussion of national balance of payments adjustment policies."[7]

Under Article 3(b) states pledge to "keep each other informed" and "consult together on a continuing basis." Through its maze of committees and working groups, and the casual rendezvous that occur on their margins, the OECD is an institutional space that fosters networks of key decision makers. By facilitating the exchange of experiences and ideas meetings at the OECD mitigate the uncertainties associated with complex governance problems and, given time, may transform the perception of those problems and their means of resolution. As Richard Eccleston has suggested, "arguably the OECD's greatest contribution to global governance....has been to host so called 'generative regimes' in which policy experts from member states can discuss policy problems and work towards developing agreed solutions."[8]

OECD meetings customarily bring together near identical conclaves of senior policymakers blending them into transgovernmental networks revolving around specific policy domains. Through exchanges of information in these settings participants learn from and about each other. This may result in policy transfer as states look to apply in their domestic context practices that have been shown to work elsewhere or the adaptation of strategy based on a better understanding of the preferences of others. Repeated interactions at the OECD inculcate officials with "the habit of cooperation"[9] where "a continuous awareness of the foreign impact of a country's policies can suffuse future policy choices and reduce the danger of actions inimical to others."[10]

Personal contacts made through the OECD also build amity and trust leading to "a better understanding of one country's policies by responsible officials in other countries, and the anticipation of a more sympathetic response......Participants in OECD meetings agree that this intangible element has given them much better insight and influenced their thinking materially."[11] By providing openings to forewarn colleagues of impending policy changes or departures from agreed positions, these channels of communication allow for "informed divergence"[12] and avoid sudden surprises that may otherwise lead to public spats. The sense of collegiality bred between bureaucrats may also contribute to slightly more flexible bargaining behavior.

Conversations stimulated at the OECD can also be the precursor to attempts to promote the "coordinated action" promised by Article 3(c) of the Convention. Before states can engage in the bargaining necessary to reach formal cooperative agreements however, they must share a baseline grasp of the nature and scope of the puzzle. Divergent or stunted comprehensions of the problem at hand often obscure the mutual interests of states. Even without this, dissonance about the intricacies of the problem and, hence, plausible solutions might still impair cooperation. Aided by the common language and statistical inputs from the secretariat, discussions at the OECD play a critical role as a discovery process where states broker the "consensual knowledge"[13] needed to frame the issue and the mutual benefits that may stem from addressing it. Given the complexity of most global governance problems and incomplete information about the costs and benefits of alternative strategies, OECD deliberations help states to identify "salient solutions"[14] around which they can coalesce and bargain. The power of states primarily determines the results of the bargaining process; as such the OECD is frequently depicted as a site for the exercise of US hegemony.[15] Bargaining culminates with the codification of consensus into legal texts concluded within the OECD framework.

The Achilles Heel of international agreements is compliance. Rationalists believe that states agree and follow international norms and rules when, based on a rational calculation of costs and benefits, it is in their interests to do so. However, this gives states the incentive to be "free riders" that avoid the costs of adjusting their own behavior but still benefit from the adjustments made by others. International organizations mitigate this through material enticements that alter the cost-benefit calculations of self-interested actors. As the OECD has no direct sanctions or enforcement instruments at its disposal, it summons surveillance mechanisms that provide information about the performance of states in relation to their promises. The OECD's peer reviews (see Box 3.1) mainly provide "systematic examination and assessment of the performance"[16] of individual states, while a multitude of scoreboards, dashboards, rankings, and benchmarks allow their conduct to be compared. Transparency deters defection by raising its costs. Knowing that they will caught, states calculate that any short-term benefits from defection will be outweighed by the longer term costs of the cooperation foregone, not least as reneging inflicts reputational damage which may harm the prospects of related OECD collaborations from which they might profit.

Equally the rationalists perceived strict limits on the OECD's ability to affect state behavior. The overwhelming majority of legal agreements concluded at the OECD take the form of soft law (see Chapter 3) under which the obligations of states are neither precise nor legally binding. The provisions of even legally binding agreements such as the OECD Convention on Combating Bribery of Foreign Public Officials in International Business Transactions "are notably generic and unspecific."[17] Indeed, "it is a marked characteristic of OECD activities that all parties take great care that recommendations or resolutions.......of the organization will not limit their freedom of action in any manner."[18] Unsurprisingly, many surveys reveal low levels of compliance with OECD ordinances. For instance, Transparency International reports that only 4 out of its 44 signatories actively enforce the anti-bribery convention and 34 have limited, little, or no enforcement.[19] The reliance on moral suasion rather than material punishments for transgressors means the OECD's surveillance is a weak reed.

As the examples of trade in services (see Chapter 1) and hazardous wastes (see Chapter 2) demonstrate, it is worth emphasizing that the consensus and soft laws attained at the OECD often become the nucleus of hard laws adopted elsewhere. That states are amenable to conferring on topics in the OECD when they will not do so in other symposia frequently reflects their appreciation that the verdict will not be codified or, if it is, that the result will be sufficiently ambiguous to tolerate legitimate differences and entail soft obligations. In doing so, these initiatives may prompt modest shifts in state conduct and lower or remove some of the informational barriers to full-fledged treaties because the "voluntary acceptance of moral obligations is often the beginning of an endogenous process in which sovereign states change their behavior over time and end up by accepting binding rules."[20] Equally, as in the case of the OECD's work on CFC's and the depletion of the ozone layer (see Chapter 2), its informal standards provide pre-cooked protocols when events trigger a sudden need for concerted international action.

Overall, the rationalist view holds that the OECD helps states to facilitate convergent policy goals, enunciate norms, and adopt legal covenants to govern their behavior. Linked to Article 3(a) and 3(b) of the Convention, the majority of OECD work is confined to the first and second of these activities. Only rarely does this lead to outbreaks of international law or the kinds of collaborative action envisaged in Article 3(c). When agreements are struck, they are normally soft laws comprising loose commitments and toothless enforcement powers. As such, they elicit minimal changes to state behavior. The content of OECD agreements and any impacts witnessed are ultimately traceable to the power of states whose interests the organization aggregated. From this, the rationalists conclude that the OECD is merely a weathervane or "benign handmaiden"[21] whose impact on global governance was imperceptible. At most, the OECD offered "air-conditioned or heated rooms, translation and secretarial services, and some rules to structure the clash or concurrence of the interests of their members."[22]

More than a weathervane?

The rationalist view of the OECD is not so much incorrect as incomplete. As the examples dotted through this book attest, states regularly select the OECD as a locale for the reconciliation of their interests and grope toward norms and rules to govern disputes arising from interdependence and globalization. With the United States initiating and shepherding "most initiatives at the OECD,"[23] the organization's pronouncements, moreover, carry the imprints of material power. Similarly, as Chapter 2 noted, the OECD's collective tonnage in the global economy means the organization's edicts often comprise the leading source of international rules to govern particular problems. In a world where international cooperation cannot be taken for granted, this alone is a worthwhile contribution to global governance. There are, nevertheless, many aspects of the OECD's work that rationalist approaches do not fully capture or explain.

First, it provides a limited appreciation of the *types* of cooperation at the OECD. Rationalist views fixate on formal OECD treaties and agreements, but the bulk of the OECD's cooperative activities are deliberative rather than decisional. As former secretary-general van Lennep declared, "ninety-nine percent of our work concerns the exchange of experience and the elaboration of lines of action."[24] Consensual knowledge from these discussions may never become international law, but it is disseminated through OECD publications, themselves important statements of cooperation against which the performance of states is contemplated. In reality, peer reviews direct much of their attention toward the broad alignment of states with generic advice contained in these documents rather than assessing compliance with formal OECD texts.

This relates to a second shortcoming, namely understating the *impact* of OECD cooperation. Despite the absence of material inducements or sanctions, the empirical evidence suggests that many states (including non-member countries) *do* adapt their behavior and become more compliant with OECD standards. For all the failings of the anti-bribery convention, it is worth asking why four countries do actively enforce the convention and another nine do so moderately.[25] Similarly, although OECD countries are regularly upbraided for the miserliness of their ODA, they have met targets related to the softening of aid terms and reductions in tied aid.[26] Furthermore, compliance with OECD directives is only one mechanism through which the organization's activities might be felt. For instance, the exchange of information and experience that is innate to the OECD way of working may lead to policy transfer as participants look to emulate at home policies that have proven successful in kindred contexts.

Lastly, rationalist accounts struggle to explain many of the *topics* under the OECD's jurisdiction. In arenas where interdependence is endemic, such as macroeconomic policy, the actions of one state have consequences for others. Under these conditions it is relatively easy to explain why rational utility maximizing actors may conclude that coordinating their policies at the OECD will produce superior outcomes to those pursued in isolation. Yet, interdependence is a negligible factor in many of the topics states explore at the OECD including education, science, health, well-being, and public sector reform. Given that education policies are impervious and insensitive to those pursued elsewhere, there seems little prospect of states making material gains from education cooperation.

OECD 2.0—A weather maker in global governance

Seeing it as an independent actor that is more than the sum of its member state parts, constructivist analyses of the OECD regard it as a weather maker whose endeavors alter the course of global governance. This interpretation centers on a vision of the OECD as a producer, and venue for the dissemination, of authoritative knowledge and ideas about the world. Rationalists perceive international cooperation predominantly as a bargaining process, treating the knowledge produced at or by the OECD merely as information to assist states to coordinate their interests or check compliance with their commitments. In contrast, constructivists see international cooperation as a social process with exposure to, and deliberation over, ideas and knowledge at the OECD helping states to learn about their world and actively constructing their interests and identities. Homage to OECD ideas and knowledge rests on their authority whose provenance lies in the expertise possessed by the secretariat and the participants in the organization's committee system. Drawing upon their professional training, these expert networks define the parameters of an issue, the angle from which to view it, the terminology to describe it, and the preferred way to tackle it. As such, international organizations like the OECD are "empowered to decide if there is a problem at all, what kind of problem it is, and whose responsibility it is to solve it.......[and] thus help to determine the kind of world that is to be governed and set the agenda for global governance."[27] For the avoidance of doubt, the constructivist argument is not that a power crazed OECD is running amok, riding roughshod over the interests of states or dictating to them what their interests should be. Rather, their point is to highlight the OECD's potential to influence global governance by acting with a degree of autonomy from its member states.

The leeway for autonomous action by OECD staff stems from the quirks of the Convention (see Introduction) and the organization's administrative structures. Acting on impulses generated by the Council and OECD committees the organization's permanent staff is, theoretically, the member's servant. Through their representatives in OECD bodies and their financial power, states do keep a firm grip on the OECD tiller (see Chapter 3). Nevertheless, "these formal arrangements leave many opportunities for the OECD administration to initiate policies, even in the absence of relevant member state claims."[28] Former OECD employees hint that states tacitly endorse this, with one noting that "if the secretariat is to be fully effective, it has to go beyond simply responding to what governments ask of it: it has to exercise imagination and resourcefulness."[29]

Reflecting the compromises needed to secure approval, the missives filtering down from members through the PWB are often couched in general terms leaving ample room for interpretation by the secretariat. Exemplified by projects such as the International Futures Programme (superseded in 2013 by the Strategic Foresight Unit operating out of the Office of the Secretary-General) and NAEC (see Chapter 2), many major OECD initiatives equip the secretariat with a horizon scanning mandate perhaps to detect challenges with long lead times or make intellectual leaps and linkages between topics, variables and disciplines. What is spotted on the horizon and whether it is deemed noteworthy depends on who is wielding the telescope and where they aim it, possibly leading the project in directions unanticipated by states. Assisted by close connections with national capitals, the secretariat also monitors domestic policy debates. Upon discovering a groundswell of ideas, it acts as an "ideational agent"[30] gathering them up before repackaging as, or coupling them to, topics alluring to member states. As one OECD official recently put it, "you have a number of areas [that] you think member states would not necessarily or spontaneously ask you [to work on], but you can build a case for the relevance of such work to their national priorities."[31] Moreover, the secretariat may behave as an "ideational artist,"[32] which floats ideas of its own. As a "laboratory of policy concepts"[33] the OECD contrives, tests and disseminates to their audience ideas about relevant issues and the means to tackle them. As one long time Director-General for Scientific Affairs at the OECD comments:

> our policy was roughly that we should be at least five years ahead of the thinking of the nation-states; second, however, we should never appear to be more than two years ahead. Otherwise, we would be killed! Our policy was to look at everything that is new, at speculative matters, matters of uncertainty……when we were successful and the nation-states would get interested, we had completed our catalytic role. We would drop these activities and begin new ones[34]

Using its bureaucratic ingenuity, the secretariat also seeks to maximize the impact of its ideas by deploying them at moments when states are most receptive to them. For instance, allied to a gathering ecological movement, the industrial unrest and student protests of 1968 provided an opportune moment for the OECD to further its ambitions in governing environmental issues.[35] Meanwhile, the 2008 global financial crisis was exploited to kick start dormant work on tax transparency (see Chapter 6).

Importantly, the problems flagged by the OECD are not just "out there" waiting to be discovered, but are actively constructed by its data and analysis. This speaks to the OECD's ability to transform "social facts" into "governable issues."[36] For example, in the early 1990s, high structural unemployment was a fact of life for many member economies, but it was the OECD's analysis that turned this into a problem of inefficient labor markets susceptible to governance by the organization's Job Strategy (see Chapter 2). Concurrently, the OECD also invents new concepts and measurements to categorize social actions. Financial assistance to developing countries predates the OECD, but it was the organization's statistical and conceptual work that determines which of this money counts as ODA. The OECD is especially adept at manipulating data to impose order on a messy complexity. By boiling issues down to a single number or measurement through its indicators and rankings, the OECD can alter the problems that are visible to policy makers and the public.

The OECD's knowledge and ideas do not exist in a vacuum but are filtered and fanned out by interactions in its political structures. In most cases, the OECD secretariat is not daubing on a blank canvas. Committee participants, especially in longstanding policy areas, may well arrive with preconceived ideas. Nevertheless, the OECD secretariat's diagnosis provides a point of departure for committee discussions plus shared concepts to describe and data to quantify the task at hand. Gradually, these measurements and conceptual vocabulary begin to be adopted as the new way of thinking and talking about a topic. Encounters with these ideas may also reshape the interests of states and constitute new actors. Instead of regarding the interests of states as the preordained corollary of material structures, constructivists believe that they emerge through deliberative processes of social interaction. By pondering new ideas with their professional counterparts, policymakers learn about the issues their country has an interest in solving, possibly also transforming perceptions about the appropriate role of the state and its institutional make up. The OECD's involvement in development and the environment not only helped to mainstream these topics in domestic politics but also, owing to the need to coordinate inputs to or national positions in the OECD, the creation of new domestic agencies and ministries to oversee them.

Expertise is the foundation of the OECD's authority, but the organization's impact on global policymaking is a function of its institutionalized relationship with senior officials from member states and beyond. What sets the OECD apart from the other major institutions of global economic governance, are the exhaustive opportunities it offers for officials to network with their professional counterparts. Repeated interactions at the OECD socialize participants into epistemic communities of "professionals with recognized expertise and competence in a particular domain and an authoritative claim to policy-relevant knowledge within that domain or issue area."[37] Steered by their professional training, principally economics in the case of the OECD, these communities share worldviews and causal beliefs that affect the problems discernible to them and the merits of alternative solutions. As the first OECD Secretary-General put it, the purpose of OECD deliberations was to create a "common value system at the level of civil servants in OECD countries that should form the basis for consensually shared definitions of problems and solutions in economic policymaking"[38].

There are a number of routes by which the collective intelligence of these networks permeates national debates. First, officials from epistemic communities may operate as "national reform entrepreneurs"[39] touting in their homeland ideas pilfered from their peer group. Enlightened by conversations at the OECD and stamped with the hallmark of international consensus, these individuals use their superior knowledge to prevail over those favoring competing policies. Australia's Treasury, for example, used the findings of OECD Surveys to lobby for the introduction of a Goods and Services Tax.[40] Conversely, national officials and agencies may sponsor activities at the OECD to overcome domestic logjams. In the 1990s, the Japanese Environment Agency patronized OECD research on extended producer responsibility (the extent to which producers should be answerable for consumption effects of their merchandise) in the hope of obtaining authoritative international endorsement to bolster an agenda they were pushing domestically.[41] Similarly, exasperation at the sluggish pace of public management reform prompted Ireland's civil service to invite an OECD peer review of its regulatory reforms.[42] Second, OECD networks facilitate transnational coalitions that can help national agencies to outwit opposition or tip the balance of domestic debates. By agitating for national strategies on, among other things, science, development cooperation, and energy, the OECD has bolstered the position of those agencies representing these areas in vying for resources. Likewise, in the 1970s, domestic agencies urging the adoption of nuclear fuels in response to the energy crisis drew upon support from the network of colleagues centered on the IEA to head off opposition from countervailing epistemic communities concerned about nuclear proliferation and accidents.[43]

Positioned upstream and downstream of them, the OECD's knowledge also pollinates debates and activities in other global institutions. The OECD's diagnostic tools and standards are widely used by other governance forums. Its Principles of Corporate Governance, now co-owned with the G20, are among the Financial Stability Board's 12 Key Standards for Sound Financial Systems and choreograph the corporate governance element of the World Bank/IMF Reports on the Observance of Standards and Codes. OECD indices are the nucleus of the analysis in many of the G20's working groups and its standards are increasingly being rolled out through engagement with non-members and third party organizations[44] (see also Chapter 6). The OECD's unpretentious work in fleshing out issues and building consensus helps to forestall gridlocks, soothe flashpoints, and pave the way toward agreements and treaties completed elsewhere (see Chapters 1 and 2). Indeed, Nicholas Bayne, the U.K.'s permanent representative to the OECD from 1985 to 1988, has fittingly christened the OECD as the "Cinderella amongst international organizations….it does not always go to the balls like its grander sister organizations, though it often runs up their dresses and sometimes clears up the mess after the party."[45]

As discussed earlier in the chapter, the outputs from the OECD way of working seldom have legal standing and, where they do, are mainly non-binding forms of soft law. Nevertheless, these instruments are potent statements of the norms around which the expectations of OECD members converge. These norms become central to the identities of OECD states reconstituting their role and perceptions of appropriate standards of behavior. The OECD's identity rests on the perception, held by members and non-members alike, that it is a club to which the world's leading states belong. The material benefits of OECD membership are arguably secondary to the status it confers. Japan's Prime Minister suggested that OECD accession showed that his country had "joined the advanced international community both in name and in fact."[46] Almost fifty years later, Colombia's finance minister described the invitation to commence OECD accession as a "step towards modernity."[47] That OECD countries are typically richer, more economically developed, and politically stable, then their non-OECD counterparts (see Table I.1) help to legitimize the organization's norms as beacons for others to follow. As Thorkil Kristensen observed, OECD countries "have been forerunners in economic development; and they will remain for a long time the pioneers in a number of fields……They can, therefore, develop certain techniques of economic policy-making that can later be transferred to other parts of the world."[48] In other words, the OECD embodies the norms and behaviors that states wishing to be regarded as "leading," "modern," or "advanced" should embrace. This also helps to explain why states, including many non-members, comply with the organization's standards.

The OECD is often dismissed as an organization with a bark but no bite. While the barks emitted by its extensive surveillance systems can draw attention to cases where states abrogate their commitments, the OECD ultimately lacks the financial or legal bite to compel changes in behavior. If material forces were the sole motivator of state behavior, this may be the end of the story, but constructivists suggest that states are also sentient actors stirred to perform in accordance with social norms for actors with a given identity. Under these circumstances, the OECD's "bark is the bite,"[49] because it signals to the international community behavior that falls short of its standards thereby damaging the reputation and credibility of the actor responsible. The OECD's dearth of material resources is offset by the ample moral resources it can deploy to shame states into conformity with community norms. The best example of this remains the OECD peer review process (see Box 3.1) where delegates regularly report experiencing, or witnessing other delegates experience, social pressure to comply.[50] The point is not necessarily that this induces among states a slavish adherence but, in feeling compelled to justify why the "correct" policies have not been followed, that they confirm OECD standards as something legitimate that they ought to be working toward. Peer reviews are augmented by a thicket of scoreboards, dashboards, benchmarks, blacklists, and rankings that enable countries to be compared not only against an OECD "ideal" but also against each other. In an organization whose members purport to be leaders, these indicators stigmatize poor performers as laggards and "configure reputational incentives for national policymakers to achieve a better score."[51]

The important thing about OECD surveillance is its visibility, revealing non-compliance or underperformance not just to peers but also to domestic audiences. Departures from OECD best practice or weak showings in OECD rankings are frequently commandeered by those petitioning for reform. DAC peer reviews, for example, are instrumental in strengthening the hand of those seeking to expand the volume or generosity of international development assistance.[52] Similarly, governments have been shamed into action by adverse publicity arising from companies falling short of the OECD's Guidelines on Multinational Enterprises.[53] Evidence from OECD surveillance may also be capitalized on to "validate policy choices whose origins lie in the preferences of domestic political actors."[54] For instance, in 2012, the French Education Minister forewarned of a drop in the country's PISA results alerting the media to their salience. When the results duly arrived the storm whipped up by the press provided a pretext for revamping the education system along the lines he had already planned.[55]

Conclusion

At a symposium marking the OECD's thirtieth anniversary Sylvia Ostry, head of the Department of Economics and Statistics from 1979 to 1983, remarked that "a great advantage of the OECD is that it has no power but great influence."[56] Blessed with only limited legal competences, no money to lend or troops to deploy it is certainly true to say that the OECD lacks recourse to material powers. Yet, the fact that the OECD is widely seen as wielding influence is prima facie evidence that it exerts power in global governance.

In this chapter, it has been suggested that ideas and knowledge are the OECD's main source of power, albeit there are contrasting perspectives about how and why the organization's ideas and knowledge are important. One version holds that the OECD is a platform exploited by members for the promotion of their interests. The knowledge the OECD provides assists states to reconcile their interests, negotiate cooperative agreements and monitor their implementation. According to this perspective, the OECD is important in fomenting international cooperation but has no independent impact on world affairs. This is now complemented by a second view that holds that the OECD's knowledge and ideas structure the way that states perceive the world, their interests and how they should act upon them. Grounded in the expertise of its secretariat and the networks which coalesce around its committee system the OECD, moreover, has a degree of independence from its members allowing it "significant discretion in its choice of topics, the way it tackles policy problems, and even in the degree of influence on policy implementation."[57] Irrespective of the viewpoint taken, perhaps "the most important thing that changes because of the OECD might be the thinking of the people involved."[58] The next chapter considers how the OECD is affecting thinking across some of the most pressing issues of global governance.

Notes

1 Quoted in Matthias Schmelzer, *The Hegemony of Growth: The OECD and the Making of the Economic Growth Paradigm* (Cambridge: Cambridge University Press, 2016), 68.
2 Nicholas Bayne, *Hanging in There: The G7 and G8 Summit in Maturity and Renewal* (Aldershot: Ashgate, 2000), 48.
3 Klaus Armingeon and Michelle Beyeler, eds., *The OECD and European Welfare States* (Cheltenham: Edward Elgar, 2004).
4 Rianne Mahon and Stephen McBride, "Standardizing and Disseminating Knowledge: The Role of the OECD in Global Governance," *European Political Science Review* 1, no. 1 (2009): 83–101.
5 See, for example, David J. Blair, *Trade Negotiations in the OECD: Structures, Institutions and States* (London: Kegan Paul International, 1993).
6 Jean-Marc Coicaud, "The OECD as a Global Data Collection and Policy Analysis Organization: Some Strengths and Weaknesses," *Global Policy* 2, no. 3 (2011): 313–14.

7 Robert W. Russell, "Transgovernmental Interaction in the International Monetary System, 1960–1972," *International Organization* 27, no. 4 (1973): 439.
8 Richard Eccleston, *The Dynamics of Global Economic Governance: The Financial Crisis, the OECD and the Politics of International Tax Cooperation* (Cheltenham: Edward Elgar, 2012), 43.
9 Michael Palmer and John Lambert et al. eds., *European Unity: A Survey of the European Institutions* (London: George Allen & Unwin, 1968), 109.
10 Henry G. Aubrey, *Atlantic Economic Cooperation: The Case of the OECD* (New York: Frederick A. Praeger, 1967), 28.
11 Ibid., 144.
12 Anne-Marie Slaughter, *A New World Order* (Princeton, N.J.: Princeton University Press, 2004), 171–72.
13 Robert L. Rothstein, "Consensual knowledge and international collaboration: some lessons from the commodity negotiations," *International Organization* 38, no. 4 (1984): 733–62.
14 Oran R. Young, "The Politics of International Regime Formation: Managing Natural Resources and the Environment," *International Organization* 43, no. 3 (1989): 369.
15 For example see Blair, *Trade Negotiations in the OECD: Structures, Institutions and States*; Miriam Camps, *"First World" Relationships: The Role of the OECD* (Paris: The Atlantic Institute for International Affairs, 1975).
16 Fabricio Pagani, "Peer Review as a Tool for Co-operation and Change," *African Security Review* 11, no. 4 (2002): 15.
17 Andrew Tyler, "Enforcing Enforcement: Is the OECD Anti-Bribery Convention's Peer Review Effective?," *George Washington International Law Review* 43, no. 1 (2011): 147.
18 Michael Henderson, "The OECD as an Instrument of National Policy," *International Journal* 36, no. 4 (1981): 793.
19 Transparency International, *Exporting Corruption: Progress report 2020: assessing enforcement of the OECD Anti-Bribery Convention*, https://issuu.com/transparencyinternational/docs/exporting_corruption_2020, 11–15.
20 Willem Molle, *Governing the World Economy* (Abingdon: Routledge, 2014), 63.
21 Richard Eccleston, "The OECD and Global Economic Governance," *Australian Journal of International Affairs* 65, no. 2 (2011): 244.
22 Thomas Nowotny, *Diplomacy and Global Governance: The Diplomatic Service in an Age of Worldwide Interdependence* (New Brunswick, N.J.: Transaction Publishers, 2011), 118.
23 Henderson, "The OECD as an Instrument of National Policy," 812.
24 Emile van Lennep, "The Interdependence of Nations and the Peace of Canada," Address to the Joint Meeting of the Canadian Club of Toronto and The Empire Club of Canada, 22 October 1973.
25 Transparency International, *Exporting Corruption: Progress report 2020: assessing enforcement of the OECD Anti-Bribery Convention*, 11–15.
26 Steven W. Hook and Jessie G. Rumsey, "The Development Aid Regime at Fifty: Policy Challenges Inside and Out," *International Studies Perspectives* 17, no. 1 (2016): 60–66.

27 Michael Barnett and Martha Finnemore, *Rules for the World: International Organizations in Global Politics* (Ithaca, N.J.: Cornell University Press, 2004), 7.
28 Jan Enkler, Sylvia Schmidt, Steffen Eckhard, Christoph Knill and Stephan Grohs, "Administrative Styles in the OECD: Bureaucratic Policy-Making beyond Formal Rules," *International Journal of Public Administration* 40, no. 8 (2017): 642.
29 David Henderson, "International Economic Cooperation Revisited," *Government and Opposition* 28, no. 1 (1993): 23–4.
30 Martin Marcussen, "The Organization for Economic Cooperation and Development as ideational artist and arbitrator: Reality or dream?," in *Decision Making Within International Organizations*, eds. Bob Renalda and Bertjan Verbeek (London: Routledge, 2004), 101.
31 Quoted in Enkler, Schmidt, Eckhard, Knill and Grohs, "Administrative Styles in the OECD: Bureaucratic Policy-Making beyond Formal Rules," 642.
32 Marcussen, "The Organization for Economic Cooperation and Development as ideational artist and arbitrator: Reality or dream?," 90–105.
33 Scott Sullivan, *From War to Wealth: Fifty Years of Innovation* (Paris: OECD, 1997), 6.
34 Alexander King, "Interview: Club of Rome founder Alexander King discusses his goals and operations," *Executive Intelligence Review* 8, no. 25 (1981): 19.
35 Schmelzer, *The Hegemony of Growth: The OECD and the Making of the Economic Growth Paradigm*, 241, 256, 288–90.
36 These phrases are borrowed respectively from Kerstin Martens and Anja P.Jakobi, "Introduction: The OECD as an Actor in International Politics," in *Mechanisms of OECD Governance: International Incentives for National Policy-Making?*, eds. Kerstin Martens and Anja P. Jakobi (Oxford: Oxford University Press, 2010), 10 and Andre Broome, Alexandra Holomar and Matthias Kranke, "Bad Science: International Organizations and the Indirect Power of Global Benchmarking," *European Journal of International Relations* 24, no. 3 (2018): 533.
37 Peter M. Haas, "Introduction: Epistemic Communities and International Policy Coordination," *International Organization* 46, no. 1 (1992): 4.
38 Thorkil Kristensen, "Five Years of O.E.C.D.," in *European Yearbook Volume XIII*, ed. The Council of Europe (The Hague: Martinus Nijhoff, 1967), 105.
39 Jarle Trondal, Martin Marcussen, Torbjörn Larsson and Frode Veggeland, *Unpacking International Organizations: Multiple Roles in Compound Bureaucracies* (Manchester: Manchester University Press, 2010), 70.
40 Richard Eccleston, *Taxing Reform: The Policies of the Consumption Tax in Japan, the United States, Canada and Australia* (Cheltenham: Edward Elgar, 2007), Chapter 3.
41 James Salzman, "Labor Rights, Globalization and Institutions: the Role and Influence of the Organization for Economic Cooperation and Development," *Michigan Journal of International Law* 21, no. 4 (2000): 778.
42 Martin Lodge, "The Importance of Being Modern: International Benchmarking and National Regulatory Innovation," *Journal of European Public Policy* 12, no. 4 (2005): 654–59.

43 Robert O. Keohane, "The International Energy Agency: State Influence and Transgovernmental Politics," *International Organization* 32, no. 4 (1978): 947–50.
44 Darryl S.L. Jarvis, "The OECD and the Reconfiguration of the State in Emerging Economies: Manufacturing 'Regulatory Capacity'," *Development and Change* 48, no. 6 (2017): 1386–1416.
45 Nicholas Bayne, "Making Sense of Western Economic Policies: The Role of the OECD," *World Today* 43, no. 2 (1987): 30.
46 Quoted in Emile van Lennep, "Japan and the OECD," *OECD Observer* no. 69 (1974): 15.
47 Johnny Crisp, "OECD Invitation 'Shows Colombia is Entering Modernity'," *Colombia Reports* 30 May 2013, https://colombiareports.com/oecd-invitation-shows-colombia-is-entering-modernity-colombia-govt/.
48 Kristensen, "Five Years of O.E.C.D.," 103–4.
49 Jason C. Sharman, "The Bark is the Bite: International Organizations and Blacklisting," *Review of International Political Economy* 16, no. 4 (2009): 573–96.
50 Hortense Jongen, "The Authority of Peer Reviews Amongst States in the Global Governance of Corruption," *Review of International Political Economy* 25, no. 6 (2018): 921–22.
51 Broome, Holomar and Kranke, "Bad Science: International Organizations and the Indirect Power of Global Benchmarking,": 533. See also Dennis Niemann and Kerstin Martens, "Soft Governance by Hard Fact? The OECD as a Knowledge Broker in Education Policy," *Global Social Policy* 18, no. 3 (2018): 274.
52 Helge Pharo, "Altruism, Security and the Impact of Oil: Norway's Foreign Economic Assistance Policy, 1958-1971," *Contemporary European History* 12, no. 4 (2003): 527–46.
53 Roger R. Blanpain, "Transnational Regulation of the Labor Relations of Multinational Enterprises," *Chicago-Kent Law Review* 58, no. 4 (1982): 927–30.
54 Stephen McBride and Russell A. Williams, "Globalization, the Restructuring of Labour Markets and Policy Convergence," *Global Social Policy* 1, no. 3 (2001): 283.
55 Bernard Hugonnier, "France and PISA: An Unfinished Dialogue," in *The Impact of the OECD on Education Worldwide*, eds. Alexander W. Wiseman and Calley Stevens Taylor (Bingley: Emerald Publishing Limited, 2017), 10.
56 Sylvia Ostry, quoted in Anonymous, "International Economic Cooperation Past and Future," *OECD Observer* no. 179 (1992–1993): S6.
57 Enkler, Schmidt, Eckhard, Knill and Grohs, "Administrative Styles in the OECD: Bureaucratic Policy-Making beyond Formal Rules,": 645.
58 Robert Wolfe, "The Organization for Economic Cooperation and Development," in *Routledge Encyclopaedia of International Political Economy*, ed. R.J.Barry Jones (London: Routledge, 2001), 1180.

5 Current issues

This chapter conveys a flavor of the OECD's contribution to global governance by sketching the issues that currently dominate its agenda. Simultaneously, a health, economic, and social crisis, the impact of the coronavirus has been felt on almost all OECD disciplines. In the short term, the coronavirus will loom large as the organization strives to assist countries to lay "the foundations for a strong, resilient, inclusive and sustainable recovery."[1] Even as its repercussions fade, the virus has given a fillip to OECD work connected with health, well-being, and technology. The crisis has likewise reiterated the necessity of cooperation with non-OECD countries, especially those of the G20. A venue for strategic engagement with the rising powers, the needs of the G20 pervades many of the OECD's work streams (see Chapters 2 and 6).

Rather than attempting to be exhaustive, the chapter is oriented around the work programs of the major OECD committees and directorates. The chapter commences with themes explicitly mentioned in the OECD Convention such as sustainable economic growth, trade, and development. It then moves on to examine topics, such as the environment, taxation, education, health, labor, and social affairs which have been elevated on the OECD agenda in recent decades (see Chapter 2). Finally, the chapter considers well-being and digitalization, two fields in which OECD engagement is relatively new, but where its authority is increasingly recognized.

Sustainable economic growth

Sustainable economic growth is the OECD's central preoccupation and the objective to which most other sectors detailed in this chapter are ultimately aimed. The ECO, by far the largest and most powerful OECD Directorate, along with the two principle committees it

DOI: 10.4324/9781351025867-6

serves, the EPC and EDRC, sets the dominant economic paradigm within which the remainder of the OECD's work program resides. Governments and the financial press eagerly await the OECD's economic policy evaluations. Accompanying the approximately 25 *Economic Surveys* released each year by the EDRC (see Chapter 3) are the OECD's other flagship economic productions, the bi-annual *Economic Outlook* and the annual *Going for Growth*. Published since 1967, the *Economic Outlook* analyses major economic trends for the next two years. Following a presentation of the global macroeconomic situation, the report turns its attention to developments in individual OECD countries and members of the G20. Started in 2005 and now traditionally launched at or on the margins of meetings of the G20 Finance Ministers and Central Bank Governors, *Going for Growth* pinpoints structural policy priorities for almost 50 countries and assesses their progress against previous iterations of the report.

Unprecedented levels of government intervention mitigated the economic fallout from the coronavirus crisis. Repeated calls for "accommodative monetary policies," cautioning against "premature and abrupt removal of [fiscal] support whilst economies are still fragile,"[2] and the watchwords of inclusiveness and sustainability suggest that the OECD will not repeat the errors of austerity. Borrowing a slogan popularized by the UN,[3] the OECD has promised a framework to "build back better"[4] by using stimulus packages to deliver a "strong, resilient, inclusive and sustainable recovery from COVID-19."[5] In response to the 2020 MCM and based on existing analytical frameworks and approaches, the Centre on Well-being, Inclusion, Sustainability and Equal Opportunity (WISE) has led the development of a dashboard of indicators to monitor, compare, and evaluate these dimensions of national level recovery programs. The dashboard includes many of the traditional barometers of progress such as GDP growth, employment and household income but also many non-material aspects of well-being. Informed by the OECD's Inclusive Growth, Wellbeing and Green Growth frameworks, these include assessing the impacts of recovery packages on the environment, equality and the ability of economies and societies to withstand future crisis.

The OECD's critics, however, regard building back better as a euphemism for business as usual. As Chapter 2 discussed, the substance of the OECD's policy recommendations is not as radical as its rhetoric. Despite nodding toward inclusivity and sustainability, for example, through support for incentivizing low-carbon investment and just transitions to low-carbon jobs, OECD documents are wedded to policies that prioritize profit and private property over human welfare and which fuel rather than dampen instability, inequality, and resource extraction. Governments are therefore advised to liberalize trade and financial markets, inject competition and flexibility into labor and product markets, upskill workers, and ensure transparent and accountable governance.[6] The coronavirus is the latest hardship exploited by the OECD as an excuse to call for states to expose their economies to global competition and to adapt their societies to meet this competitive challenge.[7] In other words, having constructed the scenario of global competition as an imperative to which countries must adapt, the OECD then sells them a package of adjustment policies. Conveniently, these entail recommendations that further embed not just a market economy but also a market society by imposing a moral framework rooted in individual responsibility and risk taking. Likewise, the OECD apparently sees no contradiction between its worries about citizens disconnecting from democratic processes and its determination to insulate economic policy making from democratic oversight. Whether the OECD is right that "revisiting fiscal rules" and "increasing the scope and independence of fiscal councils and similar institutions could help improve credibility, long-term sustainability, and transparency"[8] of public finances it also depicts a determination to place economic decision making beyond the realm of democratic governance.

Trade

A longstanding OECD aim is to maintain the openness of the international trading system by supporting the rules-based regime housed at the WTO. Although it has ceased to be an antechamber for developed countries to pre-negotiate trade issues (see Chapter 2), the OECD's data and analysis still plays a crucial role in nudging the international trade agenda forward. The OECD's work on Trade in Value Added (TiVA), Global Value Chains (GVCs), and the Services Trade Restrictiveness Index (STRI) continues to "decode the trade genome"[9] and contribute to a fuller understanding of the dynamics of trade flows. For example, approximately 70 percent of international trade involves goods crossing borders as part of GVCs. Whereas international trade statistics conventionally allocate the full value of a good to the last country in the production chain, TiVA disaggregates these figures to pinpoint where value is added.[10] In turn, this helps to provide a more accurate overview of trade imbalances and the links between trade and employment. The STRI, updated annually since commencing in 2014, quantifies obstacles to services trade across 22 sectors in 48 countries.

The OECD maintains a database of laws and regulations and, through its STRI policy simulator, allows policymakers to visualize which prohibitions are most damaging and assess the likely impact of reform policies.

By constructing internationally comparable measures of state support and modeling the effects of reforms to reduce it, the OECD hopes to build the case for trade liberalization. The OECD's presence is most pronounced in agriculture and services, arenas where it has time honored expertise, but is also seeping into other sectors typified by extensive government intervention such as semi-conductors and fossil fuels.

Between 2017 and 2019, countries monitored by the OECD granted net transfers of $619 billion to their agricultural sectors.[11] These subsidies, along with various other forms of protectionism, not only reduce and distort trade flows but also connect with other OECD concerns including environmental sustainability, income, and welfare. OECD surveillance charts changes in the levels and types of agricultural support and policy worldwide, findings that are summarized in its annual *Agricultural Policy Monitoring and Evaluation*. In conjunction with the Food and Agriculture Organization (FAO), the OECD also produces a yearly *Agricultural Outlook* assessing the prospects for various agricultural commodity markets in the decade ahead.

The focus on fossil fuels speaks to the G20's importance to the OECD trade agenda. G20 members regularly reiterate their commitment, first made in 2009, to "phase out and rationalize over the medium term inefficient fossil fuel subsidies."[12] The choice of the OECD, alongside the IEA, the World Bank, and OPEC, to investigate this issue reflected its pre-existing proficiency on subsidies in general and fossil fuels in particular.[13] Borrowing a method used to compute agricultural support, the OECD invented the notion of the Total Support Estimate (TSE) as an agreed benchmark of consumption and production subsidies. The TSE is part of a compendium of fossil fuel subsidy data jointly maintained by the OECD and IEA who, teaming up with other members of the G20 Energy Transitions Working Group, provide regular updates to the G20 about progress in eliminating subsidies.[14] The OECD Secretariat chairs peer reviews to which some G20 members voluntarily submit, giving the organization "significant influence over the definition of what constitutes a fossil fuel subsidy in the countries reviewed."[15] Fossil fuel subsidies are likewise regular ingredients of OECD *Economic Surveys* and *Environmental Performance Reviews*. The OECD also supports G20 work on trade and investment liberalization, latterly as a participant in the G20 Trade and Investment Working Group. Since 2009, the OECD, in partnership with the WTO and UNCTAD, has monitored commitments by G20 countries to refrain from initiating new trade and investment barriers publishing the associated *Reports on G20 Trade and Investment Measures* at six monthly intervals. Though no non-members subscribe to it, the OECD's Code of Liberalisation of Capital Movements (revised in 2019) is central to the G20 debate about international capital flows.

Given the OECD's and the G20's wider digitalization agenda (see below), digital trade is poised to feature prominently at the organization. Discussions of digital trade commenced in the 1990s, but in the last decade, internet connectivity has inspired new business models that are revolutionizing production processes, the scale of digital trade, and the speed of its growth. Here the OECD is reprising a role it played in preliminary discussion of trade in services. First, it is scoping out a conceptual framework to define and delimit the boundaries of digital trade. Second, it is revising statistical classification systems to make them more amenable to measuring digital trade.[16] Co-chairing (with the WTO) the Inter-Agency Task Force on International Trade Statistics, the OECD in partnership with UNCTAD, IMF, EUROSTAT, the UN, and the World Bank, curates a "living" handbook[17] of embryonic best practices for measuring digital trade, for example how to parse digitally enabled transactions from non-digital trade flows. Third, the OECD is appraising barriers to digitally enabled services including a version of STRI specifically devoted to digital services. Finally, it is unpacking regulatory issues. Digitalization blurs many of the distinctions and definitions upon which the international legal framework for trade regulation is founded.[18] WTO regulations classify products according to whether they are goods or services, but these are now bundled together in an assortment of smart devices. The geographical separation between the location of a transaction and the owner's intellectual property likewise poses questions about rules of origin.

Development

As its nomenclature and founding charter attest, sustainable worldwide development its part of the OECD's raison d'être. Almost all directorates and committees contribute to this mission, but the Development Co-operation Directorate (DCD), which supports the DAC, houses the OECD's international development specialists. The DCD seeks to stimulate and coordinate projects to hasten development, most notably with reference to the SDG's. In contrast to its more illustrious counterparts, the OECD does not possess an operational mandate in the development field. Instead through the DCD/DAC, the OECD contributes by distilling and disseminating consensual knowledge to understand, and statistical norms to quantify, development cooperation. Indeed, contemporary development discourses are replete with references to ideas, practices, and concepts, most perceptibly ODA (see Chapter 1) that originated in the DCD/DAC.

The study and analysis of development finance is the mainstay of the DCD/DAC's operation. Although it is best known for ODA, the DCD/DAC's statistical parameters encompass almost any funds with a developmental purpose such as FDI, export credits, philanthropy, and remittances. Likewise, the OECD is curious about the synergies between streams of development finance, for example, considering whether and on what basis ODA might mobilize private resources as part of blended solutions to the financing of sustainable development. The DCD/DAC also works on thematic issues, for example, the role of development finance in promoting trade, humanitarian, climate, and other sustainable development objectives. In the context of the SDGs, the DCD/DAC devotes considerable energy to defining, and then devising and refining statistical techniques to track and compute, the multiplicity of flows of development finance. Collated into the International Development Statistics online databases,[19] the OECD remains the largest and, in some areas, the only source of internationally comparable statistics about development finance.

Alongside its reputation as a statistical guru, the OECD undertakes research and analysis to maximize the effectiveness of development finance. For example, the OECD is presently examining how development finance can promote accountable and effective institutions, gender equality, and sustainable development of the world's oceans. Other projects consider how to use development finance to ameliorate the well-being of those inhabiting fragile states or conflict-prone regions, partner with CSOs in the development process, and evaluate development programs. Through their participation in these programs, development professionals advance the intellectual debate and keep the OECD in the vanguard of actors setting best practice benchmarks for bilateral aid policy. In the last five years, the OECD has authorized recommendations on the environmental assessment of development assistance projects, ending sexual exploitation, abuse, and harassment in development cooperation, the humanitarian-development-peace nexus, water governance, and managing the risk of corruption. Peer reviews, conducted approximately every six years, evaluate the member's adherence to DAC yardsticks. The OECD lubricates the wider infrastructure of global development governance by lending its statistical and analytical muscle to other bodies. Belonging to the G20

Development Working Group, the OECD actively contributes to the evolution and implementation of the G20's SDG action plan where it is presently working with the UNDP on a framework to align finance with SDG principles. In conjunction with the UNDP, the OECD provides the Secretariat of the Global Partnership for Effective Development Cooperation (GPEDC). Boasting the support of over 160 countries and 50 international organizations, the GPEDC is a "multistakeholder vehicle" that "supports practical implementation of effective development cooperation principles."[20]

The GPEDC is an outward sign of the changes being wrought to the landscape of development cooperation and the erosion of the OECD/DAC's position within it.[21] Non-DAC donors, state and non-state alike, have scaled up their development finance footprint using their wherewithal to propagate rival development paradigms and institutions. Better access to alternative sources of development finance, including private capital markets, and the shrinking number of eligible countries have diminished ODA as a source of funding for many except the poorest states. Despite DAC members being responsible for nearly 85 percent of ODA flows between 2013 and 2018[22] and disbursing $161.2 billion in 2020 alone, the DAC is also failing in its own terms. DAC members have consistently failed to meet their commitment to devote 0.7 percent of GNI to ODA. In 2020, only six of the 30 DAC members exceeded this target with the figure for DAC countries taken collectively being 0.32 percent.[23]

In a world where discussions of development cooperation are moving "beyond aid"[24] and are arbitrated by actors that lay outside its corridors, the DAC is embattled. Attempts by the OECD to adjust to the changing development habitat have exaggerated the fissures between the purist and pragmatist camps in the DAC. For the purists, the DAC's authority revolves around its aid statistics and particularly its distinctive definition of ODA. The pragmatists meanwhile insist that if it is to remain relevant to the development community, the DAC must reflect the realities of development cooperation, even if this means collaborating with actors that would weaken its like-mindedness or softening what is classified as ODA. These tensions have to come to head in the context of efforts, started in 2012, to modernize the concept of ODA. At its High Level Meeting (HLM) in 2014, the DAC committed to "undertake further work to reflect in ODA the effort of the official sector in catalyzing private sector investment in effective development."[25] Principles on these private sector instruments (PSIs) were agreed in 2016 and what remain provisional (and controversial) rules to implement them. To simplify, PSIs involve donors providing loans, equity investments, or guarantees to private companies. At issue is the fact that PSIs are offered at or near market rates. Thus, their incorporation breaches one of the cardinal principles of ODA (see Chapter 1), namely that it should entail a cost to the donor by including a minimum element of concessionality. By making the reporting rules less stringent states, led by their Finance Ministries, can inflate their levels of ODA but the effect, in the words of two former DAC Chairs, is to "undermine the basic architecture of DAC statistics"[26] and call into question its role as a gold standard for measuring progress against UN goals. They go on to note "if members continue to expand the coverage of ODA in ways that violate its basic concept and definition, we see a clear danger that the UN may in future bypass the OECD/DAC and institute its own measurement system."[27] In short, the pragmatists have the upper hand but by jeopardizing the credibility of ODA it could prove to by a pyrrhic victory. Stripped of its role as the guardian of ODA statistics, the DAC's role in global development governance would look increasingly untenable.

Environment

If the OECD Convention was rewritten, environmental aspirations would surely appear among the organization's aims. Over one-quarter of the OECD's legal acts in force concern environmental matters, and the issue is intertwined with almost every facet of its work. Incorporating energy, chemicals, air and water pollution, waste management, agricultural pesticides, cross-border pollution, recycling, noise, resource management, environmental indicators, improving the environmental performance of governance, biodiversity, development assistance cooperation, and ICT, the OECD's legal acts provide an insight into the scope of the organization's environmental remit and attempts to integrate environmental concerns into all elements of policy-making. Environmental Performance Reviews[28] are the OECD's principal mechanism for monitoring national progress in enacting these commitments and domestic environmental objectives. Environmental issues, climate change especially, also increasingly feature in *Economic Surveys* intensifying accusations that the OECD's position is "not that the economy had to function within the given environmental constraints, but the environment had to be managed within the framework of growth economics."[29]

The direct influence of OECD acts and peer reviews on national policies is secondary to their role in framing environmental problems and socializing participants into particular mindsets amenable to certain types of solution.[30] Indeed, arguably the OECD's most important contribution to global environmental governance lies in supplying the data, ideas, and technical inputs that leach into the aquifers of national policymaking and international negotiation processes. Structured around its "Pressure-State-Response" model (examining Pressures of human activities on the environment, the State of the environment and natural resources, and the Response of economic and social agents) the OECD Core Set of Environmental Indicators comprises approximately fifty internationally comparable measures of environmental performance. These are part of an encyclopedic OECD database offering barometers of, among other things, air quality, agriculture, greenhouse gas emissions, biodiversity, forest, freshwater and oceanic resources, consumption and productivity of raw materials, waste, environmental policies, expenditures, revenues and technologies. The annual *Environment at a Glance* provides a digest of the headlines arising from the indicators.[31]

Building on almost four decades of experience (see Chapter 2); the OECD continues to support climate change negotiations. The OECD and IEA provide the secretariat for the Climate Change Expert Group (CCXG) which brings together delegates from governments, civil society, and the private sector to broker common understandings of technical issues necessary to further climate change negotiations and promote implementation of the 2015 Paris Agreement.[32] For instance, the CCXG is refining the concepts necessary to finalize rules for the operation of carbon markets and to catalyze more ambitious cuts in greenhouse gas emissions. In 2021, the OECD launched its International Programme for Action on Climate to spur countries towards attaining the targets stated in the Paris Agreement. In addition to a dashboard of climate indicators, the program will provide an annual digest of country level progress toward climate objectives, dedicated reports to assist countries to develop viable national strategies, and a portal to share best practices. Elsewhere the DAC and the Research Collaborative on Tracking Finance for Climate Action are the addressing methodological and data gaps needed to "inform, accelerate and track efforts to make finance flows consistent with the goals of the Paris agreement."[33] This work, in conjunction with the OECD's wider attempts to pinpoint the policies, instruments and institutions required to scale up green investment, also feeds into the G20 Sustainable Finance Working Group.

A less celebrated, but nonetheless important, element of the OECD's environmental work is its Environment, Health and Safety Programme. Designed to inhibit trade distortions and provide a cost-effective means for governments and industry to use hazardous materials while shielding the environment and human health, its role in chemical safety "can be legitimately cited as one of the OECD's most outstanding environmental successes."[34] Given its potential dangers, the chemicals industry is tightly regulated, with governments and companies putting products through time-consuming and costly approval processes. Based on the 1981 Decision of the Council concerning the Mutual Acceptance of Data in the Assessment of Chemicals (MAD), the OECD oversees the harmonization of national procedures for chemical regulation. Signatories to MAD, including seven non-OECD members as of June 2021, agree to accept the validity of chemical safety data produced in counterparty countries, provided that it conforms to the OECD Guidelines for the Testing of Chemicals and the OECD Principles of Good Laboratory Practice.[35] In this way, the chemicals industry is spared the expense of repeating product trials for each country in which they are sold saving them €309 million per annum.[36]

Taxation

Functioning tax systems are critical to the delivery of sustainable and inclusive growth. What knits much of the OECD's tax agenda together are the perils arising from the globalization and digitalization of human activity. As well as helping governments to collect revenues that might otherwise be lost to tax avoidance and evasion, effective tax cooperation limits the recourse to unilateral actions that would inhibit growth by distorting the competitive environment and disincentivizing international trade and investment. Absent a dedicated body for this task, the OECD is often viewed as an "informal world tax organization."[37]

Topping the OECD's program is the G20 mandated work on reforming the international tax regime (see Chapter 2). Revolving around voluntary and automatic information exchange, the OECD masterminds the tax transparency agenda. The $410 billion fall in foreign owned bank deposits in offshore financial centers is at least partially attributable to voluntary tax disclosures under OECD programmes[38] which are estimated to have generated €107 billion in additional tax revenues between 2009 and 2019.[39] Since getting underway in 2017, initial assessments suggest AEOI is proving even more effective. In 2019, 97 jurisdictions exchanged information on 84 million non-resident financial accounts containing €10 trillion in assets[40] with AEOI reducing household assets stashed in tax havens by between one-fifth and two-thirds.[41] The first round of peer reviews conducted under the auspices of the Global Forum on Transparency and Exchange of Information for Tax Purposes found that 88 percent of committed jurisdictions had installed legal and regulatory frameworks that met the international standard for AEOI. Peer reviews checking whether these frameworks are implemented in practice are due to be completed by 2022. Already, new innovations are appearing to thwart the tax transparency standards and the Global Forum is likely to spend considerable time in the years ahead thinking about whether and how to close these loopholes.[42]

The OECD/G20 Inclusive Framework on BEPs oversees efforts to curtail corporate tax avoidance. Under the BEPS minimum standards, a review of which is due to be completed in 2021, almost 300 preferential tax regimes have been extinguished, 1,700 bilateral tax treaties fall within the purview of the MLI, and 90 countries have introduced country-by-country reporting requirements. Now facilitated by almost 3,000 bilateral relationships, automatic exchanges of country-by-country reports began in 2018.[43] The Inclusive Framework also continues to "address the tax challenges of the digital economy."[44] Largely unchanged since the 1920s, international tax rules broadly allocate taxing rights based on physical presence. In a world of globally integrated multinationals, operating GVCs often creating value through intangible assets, these principles are routinely abused to dodge taxes. After protracted dialogue, participants finally settled on seeking a consensus-based agreement around two pillars. Pillar one introduces a new formula that would see a greater proportion of the profits of multinational enterprises taxed in the jurisdiction of the final consumer. Pillar two implements a global minimum corporate tax rate for multinational companies. The OECD is also bringing its judgment to bear on issues including the taxation of cryptoassets and mechanisms to adjust the administration of indirect taxation in response to the emergence of the "gig economy."[45]

Tax also dovetails with the OECD's work on development and the environment. Recognizing domestic tax collection as a sustainable revenue source for governments to finance the SDGs, the OECD is engaged in a variety of capacity-building initiatives with the tax administrations of developing countries. Through the Platform for Collaboration on Tax the OECD, along with the IMF, UN and World Bank coordinates capacity building support and policy guidance for developing countries. More practically, Tax Inspectors Without Borders, run with the UNDP, sends detachments of auditors to work with their counterparts in developing countries. Together with the capacity building initiatives intrinsic to the Global Forum and the Inclusive Framework, over 30,000 officials benefitted from these activities in 2020.[46] By altering price signals, taxes are an important weapon in the armory of governments seeking to minimize environmental damage and align production and consumption choices with greener growth. Over many years, the OECD has analyzed the effectiveness of tax instruments to pursue environmental goals both in isolation and in combination with other policies. Published in the flagship triennial reports, *Effective Carbon Rates* and *Taxing Energy Use*, the OECD's work on carbon pricing, which informs the UNFCCC's annual Conference of the Parties meetings, provides an internationally accepted methodology to measure how close countries are to pricing emissions at rates reflecting their true cost to society. Jointly with the IMF, the OECD is advising the G20 on the use of carbon pricing and sketching out potential design choices for, and the impact of schemes to meet, climate mitigation pledges.[47]

Education

The OECD's Directorate for Education and Skills supports governments to design their education systems to ensure that citizens acquire the knowledge and competences required to lead a happy and successful life. Believing that better educational policies rely on strong empirical evidence, the Directorate stands at the crux of a global educational data infrastructure and "has become the recognized global provider of technical expertise in the measurement of schooling performance by governments in both member and non-member nations."[48] Data from the Directorate's research, including from presitigous surveys like PISA and PIAAC (see Chapter 2), are brought together in an annual *Education at a Glance* which provides a snapshot of the characteristics and performance of education systems in 46 countries (as of 2020). This is complemented by the EducationGPS,[49] an interactive platform integrating all the Directorate's indicators and reports. To support its inclusivity and equality agendas, the OECD is pushing the frontiers of data construction and collection. For example, with sources of educational disadvantage often embedded from a young age, the International Early Learning and Child Wellbeing Study is collating comparative data on the social, emotional, and cognitive development of five-year-olds as a basis for identifying policies to assist their learning and well-being. Complementing the assessment of their academic gifts, the Study on Social and Emotional Skills aims to prove that reliable and comparative data can be gathered on the socio-emotional competences of 10 to 15-year-olds.

A blend of benchmarking, peer learning, policy dialogue, and surveillance translate the Directorate's findings into action. Despite occasional "PISA shocks," where a sudden drop in performance relative to others inspires urgent demands for reforms in educational governance, most evaluations suggest the norms and discourses linked to the OECD percolate slowly, if sometimes profoundly, into national policymaking.[50] The effects of OECD benchmarking and analysis are amplified by peer learning events, such as the annual Education Policy Reform Dialogues, that nourish international networks of education policymakers. Countries may also opt to participate in Peer Analysis Review, one-off studies of an agreed theme involving chosen partners. Many commentators conclude that these networks have facilitated policy transfer and yielded a degree of institutional isomorphism in the education sector.[51] In terms of surveillance, the yearly *Education Policy Outlook* "is an analytical observatory that monitors the evolution of policy priorities and policy developments"[52] in the education systems of OECD countries and selected partners. Drawing upon OECD research and fieldwork, Reviews of National Policies for Education offer individual countries customized surveys and advice on educational reform.

The OECD is also tasked with assisting governments to future proof their education systems. Proposed in 2015 by the Education Policy Committee, the OECD's Future of Education and Skills 2030 scans the horizon for, and considers how education systems might mitigate, emergent challenges. Running from 2015 to 2019, the project's first phase sought to anticipate the aptitudes needed to prepare students to work with technologies and in jobs and industries yet to be invented and flesh out a common conceptual language to understand them. The second (ongoing) phase shifted the emphasis from learning to teaching looking specifically at how to produce teaching professionals and design learning environments to impart the skills needed for individuals to thrive. The various programs of the Centre for Educational Research and Innovation (CERI) also provide foresight about the educational landscape. For example, CERI's *Trends Shaping Education* appraises the meta-trends affecting education and scenarios which may arise. Connected with the OECD's digitalization theme (see below), CERI is assessing the educational implications of learning analytics, AI, and robotics.[53]

Health, labor, and social affairs

Society at a Glance is a biennial compendium of social indicators in OECD and, where available, G20 countries. Its incorporation of data on affordable housing, demographics, family, fertility, health and education expenditure, household income, inequalities, life expectancy, life satisfaction, migration, online activities, retirement, skills, social expenditure, (un)employment, violence against women and voting showcases the OECD's extensive engagement with social issues. While operating within ECO's neoliberal shadow, DELSA takes a more eclectic approach that is more receptive to the possibility that the state may play a positive role in the promotion of equality, inclusion, and social cohesion.[54] This was encapsulated in the latest (2018) statement from the OECD Ministerial Meeting on Social Policy which encouraged governments to "advance inclusive social policies that enhance economic competitiveness and productivity" but which also "support resilient social structures" and "promote more cohesive societies."[55]

Intergenerational justice and inequality tie much of DELSA's current program together. Facing persistently high unemployment, poor quality jobs, extortionate house prices, and underrepresentation in public life, many young people are at the risk of social exclusion. Utilizing its prowess on youth employment, social support, and training, the OECD updated its Youth Action Plan in 2021 that outlines concrete steps governments can implement to support young people and proposes the creation of an OECD recommendation to strengthen youth policies.[56] In cooperation with the International Labour Organization (ILO) the OECD also made a significant contribution to the G20's work on youth unemployment, including monitoring progress toward the goal, announced at the Antalya Summit of 2015, to reduce the proportion of young people at risk of being left behind in the labor market. With one in four people projected to be aged 65 or over by 2050,[57] the OECD is investigating the implications of an aging society on labor markets, healthcare systems, and retirement incomes. Given the looming pensions crisis, the OECD's data and analysis of retirement savings is playing an especially important role in ushering countries toward more sustainable pensions systems. The biennial *Pensions at a Glance* summarizes the latest developments in the pension systems of OECD and G20 countries.

OECD research shows that disparate experiences of old age materialize from another megatrend of interest to DELSA: inequality.[58] Today, studies of income, healthcare, and labor market inequalities are being joined by new concerns such as gender equality. Now over a decade old, the OECD Gender Initiative exists to monitor and press governments to embed policies to promote gender equality as enshrined in its Recommendation on Gender Equality in Education, Employment, and Entrepreneurship (2013) and Recommendation on

Gender Equality in Public Life (2015). Drawing upon data from across the OECD, the Gender Data Portal contains 75 indicators shedding light on gender inequalities in OECD and partner countries. These initiatives complement the Development Centre's Social Institutions and Gender Index which measures how laws, social norms and practices discriminate against women in 180 countries.

Alongside sustainable urban development and its effects on economic performance, inequality is also an important driver of OECD work to improve the functioning of housing markets. As a big-ticket expenditure item and the largest asset in which most people are invested, housing exerts an outsize impact on income and wealth distributions. Furthermore, a dearth of affordable housing produces secondary inequalities through limiting access to employment, schools, and public services. The outcome of a three-year-long horizontal project to build an OECD housing strategy, the OECD's Housing Policy Toolkit[59] issued at the 2021 MCM identifies indicators (consolidated into a Housing Dashboard) to compare national housing markets and polices. Work is now underway to refine the evidence base by incorporating subnational variations in house prices and more dwelling categories and to seek internationally comparable data on aspects of vulnerability such as evictions and homelessness.

The confluence of technological progress, demographic change, and globalization poses unprecedented opportunities and challenges for labor markets and healthcare systems. The diffusion of technology is facilitating the emergence of alternative business models and more flexible ways of working. While this offers the promise of additional, more productive sources of employment this is counterbalanced by anxiety about the destruction of traditional jobs, precarious employment terms, deteriorating working conditions, and the viability of social protection systems. Thus, a key strand of OECD work involves anticipating the "future of work"[60] and, through the OECD Jobs Strategy (see Chapter 2), the policies governments need to manage the reallocation of labor resources without exacerbating the polarization of labor markets. The annual *Employment Outlook* surveys the latest labor market trends and policy developments including a lengthy annex mustering statistics from the OECD Employment Database.

Over the last two decades, health has assumed a more conspicuous place in the OECD's hierarchy of concerns. Overall, the OECD's assignment is to help governments institute high performing and resilient healthcare systems that make judicious use of technology to deliver value for money and reduce health inequalities. The OECD's efforts center upon the development of statistical tools to equate the performance of diverse national health care systems. For example, the System of National Health Accounts, co-authored with the WHO and the European Commission, provides an agreed framework for reporting health care expenditures to ensure they are consistent and internationally comparable. The Health Statistics Annual Database and Health at Glance provide indicators of the health status of populations, care access, healthcare quality and outcomes, health care inputs and expenditures, pharmaceuticals, and the health workforce. Analyses such as the OECD Reviews of Public Health provide snapshots of national healthcare systems and highlight best practices. OECD best practices are increasingly contributing to the global health agenda, not least the achievement of universal health care as part of the SDGs.

Well-being

Since the inception of the Better Life Initiative in 2011, well-being has become central to the organization's remit. In 2020, the OECD created a dedicated Directorate, WISE, to coordinate its attempts to "put people and their well-being at the centre of public policy."[61] Assisted by the Statistics and Data Directorate, a central plank of WISE's activities involves providing a solid evidential foundation upon which to base policymaking discussions. Using novel data collection and analysis methodologies, the OECD has divined and refined statistical indicators that detail elements of well-being not captured by traditional macroeconomic data, including on trust, working environments, subjective well-being, and household wealth, and issued internationally agreed guidance on how to gather, interpret, disseminate, and encourage the use of these metrics. Oriented around the OECD Framework for Wellbeing and Progress, the regular publication *How's Life* uses 80 indicators to monitor well-being trends in 41 countries, while the *Better Life Index* provides an interactive tool that allows users to compare the wellbeing performance of countries. The OECD is initiating projects on topics where well-being statistics remain in their infancy. For example, to assess the well-being effects of the digital transformation, the OECD is seeking ways to overcome the absence of harmonized national data about access to and the take up of digital technologies. Likewise, it is exploring options for viable indicators to measure the impact of digital technologies on well-being touchstones including jobs and earnings, work-life balance, mental and physical health, personal security, and social connections.[62]

Informed by its concerns about inclusion and inequality, the OECD is exploring the distribution of well-being within and between social groups. Considerable work has been undertaken on intergenerational and gender well-being gaps and the issue of ethnic and racial inequality is now on WISE's radar. Concerns that well-being disparities are the sequel to childhood disadvantages have also prompted action to measure and monitor childhood well-being. Covering those up to the age of 17, the Child Wellbeing Data Portal amasses information on their family and household status, health, education, safety, and social activities to shape shared aspirations for, and related policies to promote, adolescent well-being. Another nascent theme is the nexus between well-being inequalities and the environment. Specifically, the OECD is pursuing a measurement framework that considers how environmental degradation and policies to mitigate it affect the well-being of different countries and demographic groups.[63] The OECD's work on data generation, inequality, and well-being come together in its SDG ambitions. As part of its Action Plan on the SDGs,[64] the OECD contributes to the UN's Global Indicator Framework. To this end, the OECD has hatched a methodology to chart the progress of its members against SDG targets whose results appear in the regular *Measuring Distance to the SDG Targets*. Currently, the OECD is endeavoring to taper data gaps that make assessing progress against approximately half of the SDG targets impossible.

As yet, there are few independent analyses of the impact of the OECD's well-being output on national policy frameworks, but there is growing anecdotal evidence of its impact. There is no peer review process explicitly devoted to well-being, but it is, along with the OECD's axioms of inclusivity and sustainability, bleeding slowly into the OECD's surveillance frameworks. For example, chapters on well-being are starting to appear in *Economic Surveys*. Moreover, the onset of the Better Life Initiative has coincided with an uptick in the number and complexity of initiatives by OECD governments to collate well-being data and its use to shape government decision-making.[65] Future research may well reveal how the OECD's knowledge, ideas, and standards transformed the pursuit of well-being from a fringe issue into a normal function of a modern state (see Chapter 4).

Science, technology, and digitalization

The repercussions of the digital revolution for economies and societies have been a recurring theme of this chapter. The widespread adoption of digital technologies brings both risks and opportunities. This puts the onus upon policy makers to calibrate regulatory frameworks in a way that harness the digital revolution's potential as a source of innovation, competitiveness, and political and social empowerment while mitigating the dangers and dislocations that new technologies inevitably occasion. Unfortunately, the novelty these of technologies and the dizzying speed of their evolution left policymakers without a comprehensive map of the digital landscape or a lodestar to guide them. In isolation, countries were likely to concoct governance systems that were internationally incompatible or which used regulation as a pretext for protectionism. Cognizant of the OECD's nascent prowess in this area, the G20 invited the organization to spearhead a Digital Economy Task Force which delivered a 2017 report identifying the policy challenges arising from digitalization and a roadmap to address them.[66] In parallel, the OECD finalized its own horizontal project Going Digital.

Going Digital aims to foster among policymakers a more nuanced understanding of the digital transformation, its course and impact as a basis for enacting policies to shape "a positive and inclusive digital future."[67] Initially, the project concentrated on demarcating the boundaries of the digitalization and elucidating common concepts, frameworks, and measurements through which to comprehend frontier technologies. Based on its Going Digital Integrated Policy Framework, a coordinated whole of government approach to digital governance, the OECD urged countries to adopt digital transformation strategies.[68] This was accompanied by the refinement of pristine indicators to depict the digital world as part of wider aspirations, again galvanized by the G20, to move toward a globally agreed definition of the digital economy and barometers to measure it.[69] The fruits of this work underpin annual thematic publications such as the *Digital Economy Outlook* and the *Digital Education Outlook*.

The OECD's ambition is to be "the go-to institution for 'data-on data' and a global centre for data policy."[70] As such, Going Digital's continuing attempts to fill data gaps are now accompanied by greater discussion of policy and the search for best practices. Exemplified by its work on AI, the OECD is in the vanguard of efforts to govern a host of contemporary technological problems. Jostling for leadership in the AI field, the regulatory strategies of governments have tended to prioritize investment over governance. The pace of AI innovation has outstripped that of the regulators engendering ethical and legal problems including algorithmic bias, fake news, data privacy and security, machine autonomy, and an uneven level playing field for economic competition. Now with 46 adherents, the OECD's Recommendation on Artificial Intelligence became the world's first global governance framework for AI in 2019 and the basis for the G20's AI Principles.

Launched in 2020, the OECD AI Policy Observatory provides surveillance of the principles and acts as a clearinghouse for data and analysis in 65 countries. The final phase of the Going Digital project is concerned with the governance of data. Much of this work complements what is already an impressive suite of OECD recommendations. The OECD's pioneering Guidelines on the Protection of the Privacy and Transborder Flow of Personal Data (1980) were the starting point for the data protection laws which today prevail across the OECD. Other recent landmark recommendations include those pertaining to consumer protection in e-commerce (2016), digital government strategies (2016), digital security of critical activities (2019), innovation in neurotechnology (2019), and protecting children online (2021).

Conclusion

This overview of current activities re-emphasizes many of the key characteristics of the OECD and its role in global governance. First, the OECD is an economic organization. The smorgasbord of subjects studied by the OECD is ultimately united by the desire to understand how they and their interactions affect economic life. Despite the recent tilt toward inclusivity, sustainability, and equality, the OECD's outputs are predominantly couched in terms of economic growth, competitiveness, and productivity. While it would be unfair to say that the OECD has no interest in social justice, it is regarded either as secondary concern or something best pursued via individual decisions in the market place. Second, it is as a deliberative rather than decisional forum that the OECD exerts influence over global governance. The staple activities of OECD directorates are improvising conceptual frameworks, the collection, standardization and dissemination of authoritative data, and analyzing, comparing, and distilling best practices from surveillance of national experiences. This is not to belittle the importance of OECD recommendations, but to recall they are relatively, by comparison with the volume of OECD work, few in number. Third, non-member participation in OECD activities is increasingly commonplace, something that is aiding the organization's capacity to provide global governance without global membership. Indeed, the OECD is a critical node in an array of global governance networks stretching far beyond its membership and whose perspicacity regularly make it the "go-to" institution for policymakers seeking to understand emergent issues. The next chapter ponders whether the OECD's reform program can sustain this globalization of OECD governance.

Notes

1 OECD, *2020 Ministerial Council Statement: A Strong, Resilient, Inclusive and Sustainable Recovery From COVID-19*, C/MIN(2020)7/FINAL 29 October 2020, 2.
2 OECD, *OECD Economic Outlook December 2020* (Paris: OECD, 2020), 13.
3 UN Office for Disaster Risk Reduction, *Sendai Framework for Disaster Risk Reduction 2015 – 2030*, https://www.preventionweb.net/files/43291_sendaiframeworkfordrren.pdf.
4 OECD, *Building Back Better: A Sustainable Resilient Recovery after COVID-19*, https://read.oecd-ilibrary.org/view/?ref=133_133639-s08q2ridhf&title=Building-back-better-_A-sustainable-resilient-recovery-after-Covid-19&_ga=2.177201893.1524341425.1623071473-80196136.1614014498.
5 OECD, *2020 Ministerial Council Statement: A Strong, Resilient, Inclusive and Sustainable Recovery from COVID-19*, 1.
6 See for example, OECD, *Going for Growth 2021: Shaping a Vibrant Recovery* (Paris: OECD, 2021).
7 Paul Cammack, "The OECD and the world market: antecedents of deep marketization," *Globalizations* 16, no. 6 (2019): 804–18.
8 OECD, *Meeting of the OECD Council at Ministerial Level 31 May—1 June 2021: Key Issues Paper* (Paris: OECD, 2021), 15.
9 Angel Gurria, ""21 for 21" A Proposal for Consolidation and Further Transformation of the OECD," 5 May 2015, https://www.oecd.org/about/secretary-general/21-for-21-A-Proposal-for-Consolidation-and-Further-Transformation-of-the-OECD.pdf.
10 OECD, "Trade in Value Added (TiVA): Principal Indicators," https://stats.oecd.org/Index.aspx?DataSetCode=TIVA_2018_C1.
11 OECD, *Agricultural Policy Monitoring and Evaluation 2020* (Paris: OECD, 2020), 19.
12 G20, "G20 Leaders Statement: The Pittsburgh Summit," http://www.g20.utoronto.ca/2009/2009communique0925.html.
13 Jacob Skovgaard, *The Economisation of Climate Change: How the G20, the OECD and the IMF Address Fossil Fuel Subsidies and Climate Finance* (Cambridge: Cambridge University Press, 2021), 105–18.
14 See OECD, *OECD Companion to the Inventory of Support Measures for Fossil Fuels 2021* (Paris: OECD, 2021); OECD, "OECD Work on Support for Fossil Fuels," https://www.oecd.org/fossil-fuels/.
15 Skovgaard, *The Economisation of Climate Change*, 107.
16 OECD, *Measuring the Digital Transformation* (Paris: OECD, 2019), 238–39.
17 OECD, WTO and IMF, *Handbook on Measuring Digital Trade Version 1 OECD, WTO and IMF*, https://www.oecd.org/sdd/its/Handbook-on-Measuring-Digital-Trade-Version-1.pdf.
18 R.S. Neeraj, "Trade Rules for the Digital Economy: Charting New Waters at the WTO," *World Trade Review* 18, no. S1 (2019): S121–41.
19 OECD, "International Development Statistics (IDS) Online Databases," https://www.oecd.org/dac/financing-sustainable-development/development-finance-data/idsonline.htm.
20 Global Partnership for Effective Development Cooperation, "About the Partnership," https://www.effectivecooperation.org/landing-page/about-partnership.

21 Greg Chin and Fahimul Quadir, "Introduction: Rising States, Rising Donors and the Global Aid Regime," *Third World Quarterly* 25, no. 4 (2012): 493–506.
22 OECD, "Development Finance of Countries Beyond the DAC," https://www.oecd.org/dac/dac-global-relations/non-dac-reporting.htm.
23 OECD, "Official Development Assistance 2020 – Preliminary Data," https://public.tableau.com/views/ODA_GNI/ODA2020?:language=fr&:display_count=y&publish=yes&:origin=viz_share_link?&:-showVizHome=no#1.
24 Heiner Janus, Stephan Klingebiel and Sebastian Paulo, "Beyond Aid: A Conceptual Perspective on the Transformation of Development Cooperation," *Journal of International Development* 27, no. 2 (2015): 155–69.
25 OECD, "DAC High Level Meeting Final Communiqué 16 December 2014," https://www.oecd.org/dac/OECD%20DAC%20HLM%20Communique.pdf.
26 J. Brian Atwood, Richard Manning and Hedwig Riegler, "Don't Undermine the Basic Architecture of OECD/DAC Statistics: A Letter of Warning," 21 December 2018, https://www.brookings.edu/blog/future-development/2018/12/21/dont-undermine-the-basic-architecture-of-oecd-dac-statistics-a-letter-of-warning/.
27 *Ibid.*
28 OECD, "OECD Environmental Performance Reviews," https://www.oecd-ilibrary.org/environment/oecd-environmental-performance-reviews_19900090?_ga=2.116633349.2069042008.1623665185-80196136.1614014498.
29 Matthias Schmelzer, *The Hegemony of Growth: The OECD and the Making of the Economic Growth Paradigm* (Cambridge: Cambridge University Press, 2016), 284.
30 Markku Lehtonen, "Harder Governance Built on Soft Foundations: Experience from OECD Peer Reviews," *Journal of Environmental Policy and Planning* 22, no. 6 (2020): 814–16.
31 OECD, *Environment at a Glance* (Paris: OECD, 2021).
32 OECD, "Climate Change Expert Group," https://www.oecd.org/env/cc/ccxg/.
33 OECD, *Implementing the Paris Agreement: Remaining Challenges and the Role of the OECD*, C/MIN2018(12), 2.
34 Bill L. Long, *International Environmental Issues and the OECD 1950–2000* (Paris: OECD, 2000), 124.
35 On the MAD system see OECD, *Saving Costs in Chemicals Management: How the OECD Ensures Benefits to Society* (Paris: OECD, 2019), 20–26.
36 *Ibid.*, 34.
37 Arthur J. Cockfield, "The Rise of the OECD as Informal 'World Tax Organization' Through National Responses to E-Commerce Tax Challenges," *Yale Journal of Law and Technology* 8 (2006): 136–87.
38 Pierce O'Reilly, Kevin Parra Ramirez and Michael A. Stemmer, "Exchange of Information and Bank Deposits in International Financial Centres," *OECD Taxation Working Papers No. 46* https://read.oecd-ilibrary.org/taxation/exchange-of-information-and-bank-deposits-in-international-financial-centres_025bfebe-en; Lukas Menkhoff and Jakob Miethe, "Tax Evasion in New Disguise? Examining Tax Havens' International Bank Deposits," *Journal of Public Economics* 176 (2019): 53-78;

Niels Johannesen and Gabriel Zucman, "The End of Bank Secrecy? An Evaluation of the G20 Tax Haven Crackdown," *American Economic Journal: Economic Policy* 6, no. 1 (2014): 65–91.

39 OECD Global Forum on Transparency and Exchange of Information For Tax Purposes, *Tax Transparency and Exchange of Information in Times of COVID-19* (Paris: OECD, 2020), 9.

40 OECD, *OECD Secretary-General Tax Report to G20 Finance Ministers and Central Bank Governors Italy April 2021* (Paris: OECD, 2021), 23.

41 Leo Ahrens and Fabio Bothner, "The Big Bang: Tax Evasion After Automatic Exchange of Information Under FATCA and CRS," *New Political Economy* 25, no. 6 (2020): 849–64; Sebastian Beer, Maria Delgado Coelho and Sebastien Leduc, "Hidden Treasure: The Impact of Automatic Exchange of Information on Cross-Border Tax Evasion," *IMF Working Paper WP/19/286* https://www.elibrary.imf.org/view/journals/001/2019/286/001.2019.issue-286-en.xml?language=en.

42 Menkhoff and Miethe, *ibid.*; Leo Ahrens, Lukas Hakelberg and Thomas Rixen, "A Victim of Regulatory Arbitrage? Automatic Exchange of Information and the Use of Golden Visas and Corporate Shells," *Regulation and Governance* https://onlinelibrary.wiley.com/doi/full/10.1111/rego.12363; Elisa Casi, Christoph Spengel and Barbara M.B. Stage, "Cross-border Tax Evasion after the Common Reporting Standard: Game Over?," *Journal of Public Economics* 190, no. 104240 (2020): 1–22.

43 OECD, "Activated Exchange Relationships for County-by-Country Reporting," https://www.oecd.org/tax/beps/country-by-country-exchange-relationships.htm.

44 OECD, *Addressing the Tax Challenges of the Digital Economy, Action 1 – 2015 Final Report* (Paris: OECD, 2015).

45 OECD, *Taxing Virtual Currencies: An Overview of Tax Treatments and Emerging Tax Policy Issues* (Paris: OECD, 2020); OECD, *Model Rules for Reporting by Platform Operators with respect to Sellers in the Sharing and Gig Economy* (Paris: OECD, 2021).

46 OECD, *OECD Secretary-General Tax Report to G20 Finance Ministers and Central Bank Governors Italy April 2021*, 28; Global Forum on Transparency and Exchange of Information for Tax Purposes, *Developing Capacities in Times of COVID-19* (Paris: OECD, 2021).

47 IMF/OECD, *Tax Policy and Climate Change: IMF/OECD Report for the G20 Finance Ministers and Central Bank Governors April 2021, Italy*, https://www.oecd.org/tax/tax-policy/tax-policy-and-climate-change-imf-oecd-g20-report-april-2021.pdf.

48 Sam Sellar and Bob Lingard, "The OECD and the Expansion of PISA: New Global Modes of Governance in Education," *British Educational Research Journal* 40, no. 6 (2014): 918.

49 OECD, "Education GPS: The World of Education at Your Fingertips," https://gpseducation.oecd.org/.

50 Xavier Pons, "Fifteen Years of Research on PISA Effects on Educational Governance: A Critical Review," *European Journal of Education* 52, no. 2 (2017): 131–44.

51 Alexander W. Wiseman, M. Fernanda Astiz, and David P. Baker, "Comparative Education Research Framed by Neo-institutional Theory: A Review of Diverse Approaches and Conflicting Assumptions,"

Compare: A Journal of Comparative and International Education 44, no. 5 (2014): 688–709.

52 OECD, "Education Policy Outlook," https://www.oecd.org/education/policy-outlook/.

53 OECD, *Future of Skills: Understanding the Educational Implications of AI and Robotics*, EDU/CERI/CD/RD(2019)1.

54 See for example, Rianne Mahon, "The Jobs Strategy: From neo- to Inclusive Liberalism?," *Review of International Political Economy* 18, no. 5 (2011): 570–91.

55 OECD Ministerial Meeting on Social Policy, "Social Policy for Shared Prosperity: Embracing the Future," 15 May 2018, https://www.oecd.org/social/ministerial/ministerial-statement-2018.pdf.

56 OECD, *The Updated OECD Youth Action Plan: Building Blocks for Future Action* (OECD: Paris, 2021).

57 OECD, "Historical Population Data and Projections (1950–2050)," https://stats.oecd.org/index.aspx/Index.aspx?DataSetCode=POP_PROJ.

58 OECD, *Preventing Ageing Unequally* (OECD: Paris, 2017).

59 OECD, *OECD Housing Policy Toolkit – Synthesis Report*, C/MIN(2021)5.

60 OECD, *The Future of Work: OECD Employment Outlook 2019* (Paris: OECD, 2019).

61 OECD, "Centre on Well-being, Inclusion, Sustainability and Equal Opportunity," https://www.oecd.org/wise/.

62 OECD, *How's Life in the Digital Age? Opportunities and Risks of the Digital Transformation for People's Well-being* (OECD: Paris, 2019), 121–28.

63 OECD, *The Inequalities-Environment Nexus: Towards a People-Centred Green Transition* (Paris: OECD, 2021).

64 OECD, *Better Policies for 2030: An OECD Action Plan on the Sustainable Development Goals* (Paris: OECD, 2016).

65 Carrie Exton and Michal Shinwell, "Policy Use of Well-being Metrics: Describing Countries' Experiences," *OECD Statistics Working Papers 2018/07*, https://www.oecd-ilibrary.org/deliver/d98eb8ed-en.pdf?itemId=%2Fcontent%2Fpaper%2Fd98eb8ed-en&mimeType=pdf.

66 OECD, *Key Issues for Digital Transformation in the G20: Report prepared for a joint G20 German Presidency/OECD conference Berlin, Germany 12 January 2017* (Paris: OECD, 2017); G20, "A ROADMAP for Digitalisation: Policies for a Digital Future," http://www.g20.utoronto.ca/2017/170407-digitalization-annex1.html.

67 OECD, "About the Toolkit," https://goingdigital.oecd.org/about.

68 OECD, *Going Digital: Shaping Policies, Improving Lives* (Paris: OECD, 2019).

69 OECD, *Measuring the Digital Transformation: A Roadmap for the Future* (Paris: OECD, 2019); OECD, *A Roadmap Toward A Common Framework for Measuring the Digital Economy: Report for the G20 Digital Economy Task Force* (Paris: OECD, 2020).

70 OECD, *2019 Strategic Orientations of the Secretary-General* (Paris: OECD, 2019), 8.

6 OECD reform

The 2008 financial meltdown transformed latent dissatisfaction with the system of global economic governance into a full-blown legitimacy crisis. Insofar as the cooperative ventures pursued through multilateral economic institutions prevented the crisis from metastasizing into a full-blown depression, it is feasible to claim "the system worked."[1] The crisis was nevertheless symptomatic of the malaise afflicting the multilateral economic organizations.[2] Having failed to detect the crisis, the multilateral economic institutions then compounded its consequences by imposing, or providing the intellectual cover for, austerity policies that stifled economic growth and shattered mechanisms designed to assuage inequality.[3] The 2008 crisis also accelerated the eastwards shift in the global economic (and political) center of gravity. As such, the institutions of global economic governance, anchored in the "1945 moment" and the dominant practices and priorities of the West, appeared increasingly anachronistic.

All multilateral economic organizations confronted these afflictions, but its methods, mission, and membership meant they were especially acute for the OECD. Compared with its contemporaries, the authority of the OECD's recommendations rests disproportionately on its methods of economic surveillance which, by not espying the biggest economic calamity since the 1930s, dented its reputation more seriously. Presiding over a period of economic stagnation also cast doubt on the OECD's aptitude for dispensing its core mission, namely the promotion of growth-oriented policies. The organization's claims to be the custodian of the paramount prescription for economic growth were belied by its own forecasts, which envisaged the expansion of non-member economies persistently outstripping those of the OECD.[4] The OECD countries' commensurately contracting share of almost every facet of commercial activity spills over into questions of membership. Devoid of several systemically significant economies,

DOI: 10.4324/9781351025867-7

most notably China, the OECD's membership sapped its stature as a venue for the arbitration of global economic challenges. As one former Secretary-General put it, "how are you going to shape the global economy if you're basically working with a minority of it?"[5]

To allay these brickbats the OECD is prosecuting a thoroughgoing reform program, the centerpiece of which is a Global Relations Strategy "to promote and diffuse the OECD's values, and increase the relevance and acceptance of its standards and best practices globally."[6] Three strands underpin the strategy: membership enlargement, partnership with non-members, and a sturdier OECD-G8-G20 nexus. In short, the OECD is trying to situate itself as a setting where the handshake between the dominant powers of the twentieth century and those poised to dominate the twenty first can be consummated.

The remainder of this chapter peruses the present status of the OECD reform package and its outlook for realizing the intended benefits. The next section adumbrates the OECD's attitude to enlargement, pondering how recent and prospective accessions have affected the organization's personality and performance. Attention then switches to the OECD's portfolio of non-member partnerships ranging from formal schemes targeting specific states to more generic arrangements to entice broad participation in the organization's work. The third section scrutinizes the OECD's affiliations with the G7/8 and G20. The OECD's adoption of an "a la carte"[7] approach has so far allowed it to quell contradictions in the reform process. Careful management of these conflicts is essential if the OECD is to disarm its opponents without debilitating the organization or drastically altering its temperament.

OECD enlargement

By bolstering the legitimacy and spread of the organization's outputs, membership enlargement supposedly serves to assist the OECD with the delivery of its mandate. As fresh members must embrace the OECD acquis, accession "remains the most powerful instrument to expand the reach and impact of OECD values and standards."[8] Rules adopted by a broader, more globally representative membership would be more legitimate enhancing their worldwide applicability. Moreover, the assimilation of extra states into the OECD's statistical and surveillance frameworks provides it with an enriched understanding of the global economic jigsaw as a basis for identifying and promoting the best policies to promote economic growth and rising living standards. Among the members, however, enlargement is a perennially prickly subject. Complicated by nebulous membership requirements, reservations about the ramifications of new members for the organization's effectiveness, governance, and identity have plagued every accession since Japan in 1964. Inevitably, the dialogue to admit more countries to an organization whose membership had already swelled by three-quarters since 1994 are proving "prolonged and contentious."[9]

The 2016 MCM called "for a strategic reflection by Members on the future size and membership of the Organisation."[10] Chaired by the Canadian Ambassador to the OECD, a working group was established to contemplate the composition of the membership and to formalize the organization's membership criteria. The working group's submission to the 2017 MCM did not enumerate "hard and fast rules on the ultimate size of the OECD,"[11] reporting that members were content with enlargement provided that the organization's effectiveness was unimpinged. The submission also proposed benchmarks to identify, or gauge the suitability of, prospective members.

Tentative steps in this direction had commenced with the 2004 Noburu Report which suggested accession candidates should be both "likeminded," and "significant players," whose membership would stoke "mutual benefits." A fourth factor, "'global considerations' concerned the overall balance of the membership."[12] In 2006, these yardsticks were folded into an instrument[13] to pinpoint potential members but were never codified into concrete accession criteria. Confirming the validity of the Noburu principles, plus the values and principles expounded in the 50th Anniversary Vision Statement[14] and 2013 Global Relations Strategy,[15] the OECD adopted a framework to weigh the merits of possible members.[16] The components of this framework are, firstly, an assessment of a country's "state of readiness" including the ability to traverse the accession process, custody of a prominent role in regional or global economic governance, and a willingness to observe core OECD instruments on corporate governance, good statistical practices, internet policy making, international investment and multinational enterprises, combating bribery, and the liberalization of capital movements and current invisible operations. Second, aspirant members must exhibit alignment with the OECD's "fundamental values.......of democracy based on the rule of law and human rights, and adherence to open and transparent market-economy principles."[17] Third, the country must possess adequate institutional foundations and economic governance. Fourth, the country's economic performance over the last five years is evaluated. Finally, hopeful applicants must demonstrate high-level political commitment to membership obligations through a track record of convergence with members motivated by way of involvement in OECD committees and surveillance processes.

The anticipated flurry of new members is fraught with practical and political problems, however. Following the accessions of Colombia and Costa Rica, no countries are presently undergoing the OECD membership process. Membership applications from Argentina, Brazil, Bulgaria, Croatia, Peru, and Romania are under consideration by the OECD Council. This roster epitomizes the compromises needed to secure enlargement, not least because every existing member can veto accession. Reflecting geopolitical sensitivities and the related battle over the OECD's future trajectory, disagreements about who should join and in what sequence have dogged attempts to progress membership applications. Most members are predisposed to prioritize the accession of their neighbors and allies and the larger members are generally keener to press the case of the systemically important non-member economies. Historical animosities pose further snags. For example, Hungary is blocking Romania's membership over its treatment of Hungarian minorities and Slovenia is opposing Croatia's application over a maritime border dispute.

Admission of these countries is also unlikely to assuage allegations about the OECD's illegitimacy. These states might be sufficiently "likeminded" for OECD membership but barring Brazil, the world's eighth biggest national economy by GDP (PPP),[18] they hardly constitute "significant players." Argentina (the 29th biggest economy), Romania (41st), and Peru (43rd) are middle-ranking economic powers, but Bulgaria (73rd) and Croatia (82nd) are minnows. An influx of smaller countries threatens to enlarge the OECD's membership without enlarging its influence. For example, Australia calculated that incorporating Colombia, Latvia, Costa Rica, and Lithuania would increase membership by 14 percent yet the OECD's share of global GDP would drop 4 percent because non-members, especially from Asia, were growing quicker.[19] Despite prioritizing "South East Asia with a view to identifying countries for possible membership"[20] since 2006, no country from the world's fastest advancing region has expressed serious membership ambitions. Inroads into Latin America notwithstanding, these accessions perpetuate the OECD's Euro-centric character and point to a persistently widening chasm between the geography of the OECD and that of the global economy.

The obvious solution of inviting the membership of systemically significant states is similarly problematic. These states, several now designated by the OECD as Key Partners (see below), are lukewarm about membership. The rising powers are understandably wary about fraternizing with an organization they still regard as a "rich country club" used by its members to concert their interests against 'the rest' (see Chapters 1 and 2). As well as detrimentally affecting their South-South relationships, subservience to the OECD will restrict the ability of emerging powers to exercise their newfound power by entangling them in the rules, norms, and principles of the existing liberal order. In this regard, the global giants are also disenchanted at the thought of listening to long lectures from their Lilliputian counterparts. Furthermore, their "hard' conceptions of sovereignty, which repudiate external criticism and the infringement of international institutions upon their authority, look incompatible with the intrusive nature of OECD surveillance. In short, whereas the current batch of accession states are likeminded but not significant players, the significant players are insufficiently likeminded.

Irrespective of their thirst to enlist, the possibility that the fundamental values and institutional foundations of the systemically important states will converge with those stipulated in the OECD framework for prospective members remains remote. At best, these countries might be described as having a patchy commitment to democracy, the rule of law and human rights, matters "considered as particularly important parameters for judging whether a candidate country ultimately should be invited to join OECD."[21] Likewise, the varieties of capitalism emerging in these economies, especially the state's pronounced role in undertaking commercial activity and organizing the means of production through state-owned enterprises, differ starkly from those in the OECD. A steadfast refusal to eliminate capital controls, endemic bribery and corruption, and politically manipulated statistics are just some of the institutional shortcomings that would stop these states passing muster with the gauntlet of technical assessments by OECD committees.

Regardless of the Key Partners, a growing membership entails complications for the OECD's operations and governance. Although candidate countries are meticulously vetted and the accession process catalyzes reforms that tighten their alignment with the OECD acquis, the increasing size and diversity of the membership muddies the deliberative process. The changing quarters for OECD meetings provide a salutary metaphor. Committees that once convened around a conference table in the cozy ambience of the Chateau de la Muette, now gather in the cavernous chambers of the OECD conference center. Sitting in a horseshoe configuration, the physical abyss between the interlocutors sometimes symbolizes the ideational voids between them.[22] By slowing the search for consensus an enlarged membership may nullify the gains derived from streamlining the committee system (see Chapter 2). This could rekindle debates about the timeliness of OECD advice and enfeeble its capacity to act as a caucusing body for likeminded states in the wider architecture of global governance.

Precautions are also needed to avoid overloading the OECD's surveillance systems. Even with 38 members, certain OECD committees, such as the lynchpin EDRC, are at saturation point. Attenuating the frequency or bounds of the peer reviews and other surveillance routines would alleviate this pressure but undermine the quality of advice the organization can supply to its clients. OECD surveillance is also resource intensive with every accession adding approximately one percent to its expenditure, a significant burden in the ongoing climate of budgetary stringency. Mindful that inefficiency might offset the dividends of inclusivity the OECD has expedited efforts to streamline its governance, financial and working practices. The phasing in of the financial package announced at the 2008 MCM (see Chapter 3) guarantees that new accessions pay the full costs of membership upfront. The OECD has taken steps to hasten decision making by tapering the list of categories requiring mutual agreement or unanimity thereby stretching the sphere of QMV and encouraging committees to rationalize their practices to focus attention on substantive discussion items.[23] There are, however, limits to what these innovations can achieve. For example, financial reforms must be placed in the context of a budget frozen in real terms for a decade and which, for the 2019–20 biennium, members ordered could not grow in nominal terms. Coming on top of their insistence that the OECD absorb the costs of members' pension contributions, the Secretary-General warned "our ability to cut expenses without cutting substance has reached its limits."[24]

Non-member partnerships

The OECD's desire to globalize its authority without globalizing its membership has compelled it to contrive alternative ways to immerse non-members in its work. The OECD has lasting links with non-members, but the Global Relations Strategy aims to make them more systematized, institutionalized, and democratized. As Chapter 3 outlined, the OECD asks all committees to proactively pursue non-member participation and has made it simpler for non-members to be more closely embroiled on a more consistent basis in the organization's operations. The OECD has also strived to alter the tenor of its interaction from what were sometimes perceived by non-members as patronizing monologues[25] into reciprocal dialogue. This is perceptible in the

OECD's choice of "Partners" as the term to describe all non-member participants.[26] Where possible, the OECD involves Partners in priority setting, programme management, and the resultant outputs.

At the apex of these arrangements is the OECD's interface with its Key Partners: Brazil, China, India, Indonesia, and South Africa. Through the Key Partners program, the OECD courts enhanced engagement with non-members that are significant economic players but which are loath to undertake, or unqualified for, the rigors of accession. The OECD's relations with Key Partners are distinguished from those with other countries by their formality, extensity and status. The initiative encompasses an explicit undertaking by the OECD to engage with Key Partners across the spectrum of the organization's work on the basis of near equality.[27] Programs are customized for individual countries but typically the Key Partners will attend the economic sessions of the MCM, are invited to sectoral ministerial meetings, and appear in flagship OECD publications including the *Economic Outlook* and *At a Glance* series. Likewise, in committees where they are designated as Associates (see Chapter 3) Key Partners help to develop OECD instruments and their compliance is monitored through integration into the organization's statistical and surveillance systems. This is complemented by intensified collaboration outside the OECD. For instance, the Key Partners have appointed diplomats responsible for coordinating relations with the OECD to their Paris embassies. Meanwhile, the OECD has instated offices in Jakarta and Beijing and partnered with other international economic organizations to produce reports on, or sponsor meetings in, these five countries. The OECD's vision is that through sustained exposure, the OECD's values, ideas, and standards will take root in Key Partners and stimulate the reforms necessary to make them eligible for accession. In the interregnum, the participation of sizable non-members would leaven the OECD's desirability as a venue for addressing urgent problems of global governance.

To a point, the OECD's Key Partners program is reaping rewards. Since the formal inauguration of enhanced engagement in 2007 there has, albeit unevenly, been a step change in the scope and intimacy of the OECD's relationships with Key Partners. As Figures 6.1 and 6.2 indicate, Key Partners are signing OECD instruments and participating in OECD organs and projects in record numbers. Representatives of these states are also becoming more prominent, with each Key Partner holding a vice-chair of at least one OECD body. These developments have also helped to build the OECD's rapport with the G20 (see below). The gravitation of these countries toward the OECD model is pedestrian nonetheless. Thirteen years on and the Key Partners are associated

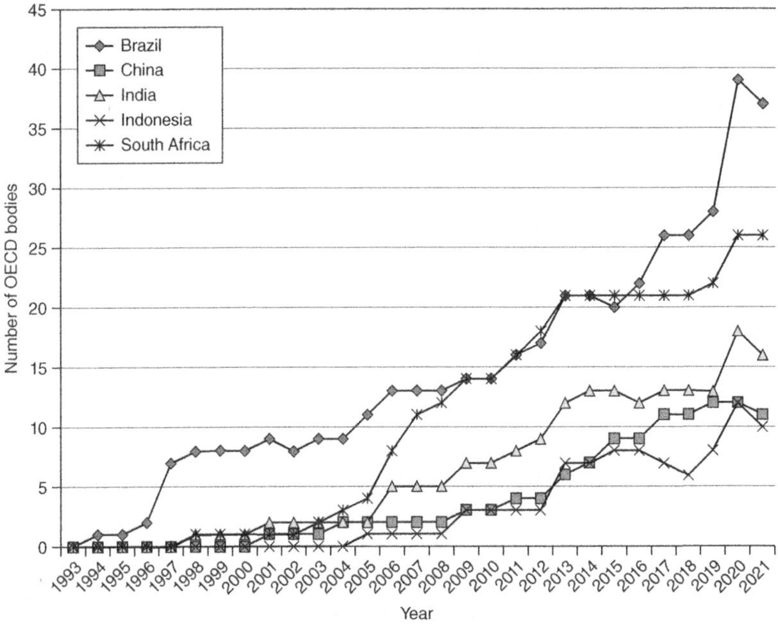

Figure 6.1 Key Partners: Partnerships in OECD bodies and projects
Source: Adapted from OECD, *The Secretary-General's Report to Ministers on Global Relations: OECD Global Relations: Serving the OECD and its Members with global impact*, C/MIN(2021)8, 8; OECD, *Making OECD Standards and Policies Count on a Global Scale*, C/MIN(2019)11, 9; OECD, *The OECD's Global Relations: Meeting the Strategic Challenges*, C/MIN(2018)8, 18.

with a minority of the OECD's work programme and, Brazil excepted, are peripheral adherents to its standards. The scantiest progress has been with China, the partner the OECD most covets because of its economic heft. For China's Ministry of Foreign Affairs, the OECD is a relatively low priority. As such, compared with the other Key Partners, China's enmeshment with the OECD has been narrow, concentrated most conspicuously in fiscal affairs, and shallow, confined to the most circumspect engagement choices.[28] Brazil, the only Key Partner to officially declare its interest in membership in 2017, could well be the litmus test for this initiative. Three years on and Brazil's application is still under consideration by the OECD Council pointing to protracted accession pathway. Despite the sudden uptick in Brazil's espousal of OECD standards (see Figure 6.2), assertions that it is imminently likely to conform to the organization's fundamental values seem far-fetched. The Russian Federation's accession, suspended in March 2014

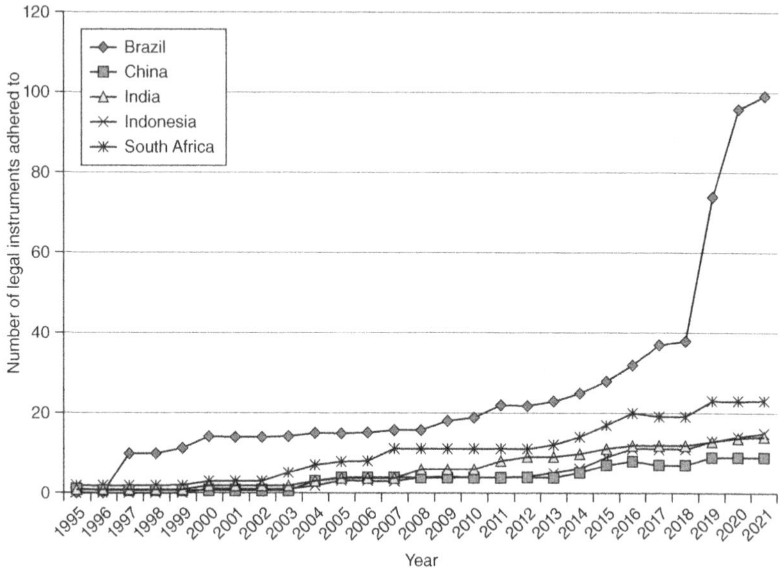

Figure 6.2 Key Partners: Adherence to OECD legal instruments
Source: Adapted from OECD, *The Secretary-General's Report to Ministers on Global Relations: OECD Global Relations: Serving the OECD and its Members with global impact*, C/MIN(2021)8, 8; OECD, *Making OECD Standards and Policies Count on a Global Scale*, C/MIN(2019)11, 9; OECD, *The OECD's Global Relations: Meeting the Strategic Challenges*, C/MIN(2018)8, 18.

following its annexation of Crimea, is a portent. The allure of membership undoubtedly catalyzed profound adjustments that modernized Russia's regulatory framework. Sadly, this was not matched by a corresponding evolution in the norms and values of Russian society. The country's clampdown on political freedoms and personal liberties, everyday violations of property rights and widespread state interference in enterprise, remained incompatible with the OECD's core ideals.[29]

Serious doubts persist about the whether the Key Partners will ever qualify for OECD membership. The OECD's claims about the power of accession to socialize states with the institution's values or otherwise cajole them into domestic reforms rests on the presumption that prospective members can be treated as supplicants. In these circumstances, the OECD can insist that entry to its hallowed club is conditional upon sufficient progress toward the organization's rules and values. This logic is not germane to the Key Partners. The truth, as its attitude toward them implicitly acknowledges, is that the OECD needs the Key Partners as much, if not more, than they need the OECD.

A suite of regional and country-level programs complement the OECD's focus on Key Partners. Taking their strategic guidance from the Council[30] and tethered in regional institutions these programs "facilitate the participation of countries from a region as a group in selected OECD activities."[31] Longstanding regional activities in the Sahel and West Africa Club (1976), South-East Europe (2000), the Middle East and North Africa (2005), and Eurasia (2008) have lately been buttressed by initiatives in Southeast Asia (2013) and Latin America and the Caribbean (2016). These additions reflect the recent recruitment of Latin American states to the OECD and the priority accorded to enrolling more Southeast Asian countries to its ranks. Initiatives are tailored to specific regions but share the overarching objectives of raising the organization's profile and emboldening domestic reforms by urging deeper absorption into OECD bodies or betrothal to its standards. They also serve as platforms through which regional international organizations coordinate relevant work with the OECD.

Today, almost all countries are involved in some aspect of the OECD's work. The majority are subsumed on a temporary and topic-specific basis. Country Programmes, in contrast, comprising renewable fixed term periods of structured cooperation with the organization, are aimed at non-members which, while not intent on membership, are nonetheless inclined toward multiple OECD standards. Each program is bespoke but is calculated to allow countries to imbibe OECD expertise, contribute to committees including the systematic exchange of information and peer review, and to dovetail with regional initiatives.[32] As well as installing standards in specific national contexts, the OECD has one eye to a wider audience trusting that these countries will act as beacons of best practice that will radiate across the region. Country programmes with Kazakhstan and Peru reached their fruition in 2018, programmes with Morocco and Thailand are ongoing, and the Council has solicited programme proposals from Egypt and Vietnam.

The OECD's Global Forums provide the most general, but with some exceptions the least influential, mechanism for non-member inclusion. Created by one or more OECD committees, Global Forums are hubs for stakeholders, including CSOs, from specific policy communities to tussle with themes transcending countries or regions especially "where the relevance of OECD work is dependent on or can be enhanced by interaction and policy dialogue with a wide range of relevant actors from various regions of the world."[33] Standing slightly apart from mainstream OECD work, Global Forums can help committees by sponsoring converging views about the nature of global problems and their prospective solutions and scanning the horizon for incipient problems. Today, 14 Global Fora cover agriculture, biotechnology, competition, development, digital security, education, environment, public debt management, productivity, public governance, responsible business conduct, tourism statistics, trade, and value-added tax.

The OECD-G7/8-G20 nexus

Despite being nested amidst jumble of interrelated regional and global bodies, the OECD's relationship with other international institutions has been neglected by scholarly researchers. Nonetheless, as Chapter 4 intimated, the OECD's data, analysis, and deliberations provide indispensable lubrication to the wider processes of global economic governance. Seeing this as another avenue for the globalization of OECD governance, the organization has lately invested considerable capital putting, what are in many cases, lifelong relationships on a firmer footing. This includes the Bretton Woods institutions, many of the UN semi-autonomous and specialized agencies, regional organizations such as APEC[34] but, aside from the EU with its quasi-membership of the OECD (see Chapter 3), has unquestionably proceeded farthest with the G7/8/20.

As improvised groups without independent secretariats, founding charters, permanent headquarters, and legal powers, the G7/8/20 draw heavily on the analytical and administrative muscle of international organizations to prepare their meetings and oversee the implementation and monitoring of commitments afterwards. Once they had overcome some initial distrust (see Chapter 1), complementarities in orientation, style, and membership made the OECD a natural partner for the G7. Lodestars for the virtues of capitalism and democracy, the G7 and OECD shared an affinity for informal dialogue rather than formal negotiation. Furthermore, the financial contributions and economic weight of the G7 members allowed them to steer work programs entrusted to the OECD.[35] As an "international economic conference in permanent session,"[36] the OECD was a convenient conduit for the G7 to maintain the momentum between their sporadic meetings. As well as commissioning new work, the G7 regularly endorsed or urged the intensification of the OECD's agenda and made pledges to cooperate within the organization. Ongoing research, analysis, and discussion at the OECD tapered fissures among G7 countries to a point where face-to-face summit meetings could bridge them.

The prospering OECD-G7/8 nexus is indicated by the proliferation of references to the former in the communiqués of the latter (see Table 6.1). For all this, the OECD's dealings with the G7/8 system "were close but often uneasy."[37] Sometimes the OECD felt snubbed by

Table 6.1 References to the OECD in G7/8 summit and ministerial communiqués and documents

	1st cycle (1975–81)	*2nd cycle (1982–88)*	*3rd cycle (1989–95)*	*4th cycle (1996–2002)*	*5th cycle (2003-2010)*	*6th cycle (2011-2018)*
Reference to OECD work or act	0	0	6	62	88	59
Welcome/endorse OECD work	7	8	16	64	75	41
Endorse and ask OECD to intensify efforts	0	1	6	15	19	11
Request/urge OECD to act	0	0	7	23	34	18
Pledge to cooperate with/in OECD	5	5	2	20	20	31
Total	12	14	37	184	236	160

Source: Derived from G7/8 communiqués published by the University of Toronto G8 Information Centre, http://www.g8.utoronto.ca/summit/index.htm and http://www.g8.utoronto.ca/meetings.html.

the G7/8. For instance, when the Okinawa Summit of 2000 established a Digital Opportunity Task Force to enable developing countries to extract a windfall from information technology, "the OECD was best placed to co-ordinate the follow-up; yet the responsibility was dispersed to other organizations with less expertise."[38] Furthermore, while the G7/8 invited the heads of other international economic organizations (including the IEA, one of the OECD's semi-autonomous bodies) to participate in their annual jamboree, it took until the Heiligendamm Summit of 2007 for the same courtesy to be extended to the OECD Secretary-General.

The 2007 Summit marked a watershed in G7/8-OECD relations. In addition to welcoming its Secretary-General the G8 selected the OECD as a platform for the Heiligendamm Process, the moniker bestowed on the G8's dialogue with the Outreach-5 countries, Brazil, China, India, Mexico, and South Africa. As the existence of the Heiligendamm Process illustrated, however, the ground was already shifting under the OECD's feet. The Heiligendamm Process had barely begun when the global financial crisis struck whereupon, to orchestrate the response, the world turned not to the G7/8 but the G20, another forum signifying the increasingly shared stewardship of the global economy between the established and the emerging powers. Founded in the wake of the Asian financial crisis, the G20 originally convened as a forum of finance ministers and central bank governors. Starting with the Washington Summit of November 2008, the G20 was elevated to the level of national leaders. At the following year's Pittsburgh Summit, the first to be attended by the OECD Secretary-General, the G20 was designated "the premier forum for our international economic cooperation."[39]

Luckily for the OECD, the G20 inherited the G7/8's institutional attributes, not least the absence of a supporting secretariat. In other words, like the G7/8, the G20 is akin to a puppeteer giving strategic impulses to an auxiliary cast of international organizations upon whom it relies for the operationalization of its commitments. The OECD's good fortune was supplemented by some deft entrepreneurialism from its Secretary-General, epitomized by the G20's embrace of the OECD's initiative to promote international tax cooperation.[40] Undeterred by disagreements that had brought its harmful tax competition initiative to a political impasse (see Chapter 2); the OECD persisted in its attempts to curb tax avoidance and evasion by encouraging national revenue authorities to exchange information with their foreign counterparts. Gurria sensed that the fallout from the financial crisis offered him the opportunity to advance the OECD agenda and shore up the organization's position in the global governance architecture. Tax havens were not directly implicated in the causes of the global financial crisis; nonetheless they made convenient bogeymen especially for states needing to staunch bloodletting on their public balance sheets. His gift-wrapped solution, in the form of an internationally agreed tax standard, was gleefully grasped by G20 leaders desperate to give the impression they were mounting a decisive response to the crisis by declaring, precipitately but trenchantly, that the "era of banking secrecy is over."[41]

In the intervening decade, the G20-OECD nexus widened and deepened through the maturation of the G20 system and institutional innovations at the OECD. In its guise as a "crisis committee," the G20 was widely credited with helping to drag the world economy away from the precipice. Once the immediate threat of financial cataclysm receded, however, the G20 started to act more as a "steering committee" providing strategic leadership and identifying priorities for the governance of the world economy.[42] Consequently, following the precedent of the G7/8, a broader range of issues soon fell within the G20's purview spawning a throng of working groups, technical committees, and ministerial meetings to which Gurria or members of his entourage were frequently invited. To enhance its responsiveness to the G7/8/20, these developments were accompanied by internal changes at the OECD. Beginning life as a temporary entity to support the Heiligendamm Process, today the Sherpa Office and Global Governance Unit is the interface between the OECD and the other multilateral economic institutions. Stationed within the office of the Secretary-General, the unit coordinates the OECD's inputs to the G7/8/20, and anticipates issues of likely interest. Dedicated members of staff, most notably a G7/8/20 Sherpa, liaise between the OECD and G7/8/20. That the organization contributes to so many strands of the G20's work (see Chapter 5) is testament not only to the latitude of the OECD's expertise but also the proactive placement of its wares in the shop window. This is reflected in burgeoning references to, affirmations of, and requests for, the OECD's work in G20 communiqués (see Figure 6.3).

The development of the OECD-G7/8/20 relationship has proceeded to a point where some believe it should be formalized with the OECD becoming a permanent secretariat to the G's.[43] Whether a permanent secretariat would help or hinder the G7/8/20's effectiveness has long been debated,[44] but such an arrangement could be advantageous to the OECD. First, the custody of a definitive role would seal the OECD's position in global governance. Second, closer ties, especially with the G20, jibe with the OECD's resolution "to better integrate the

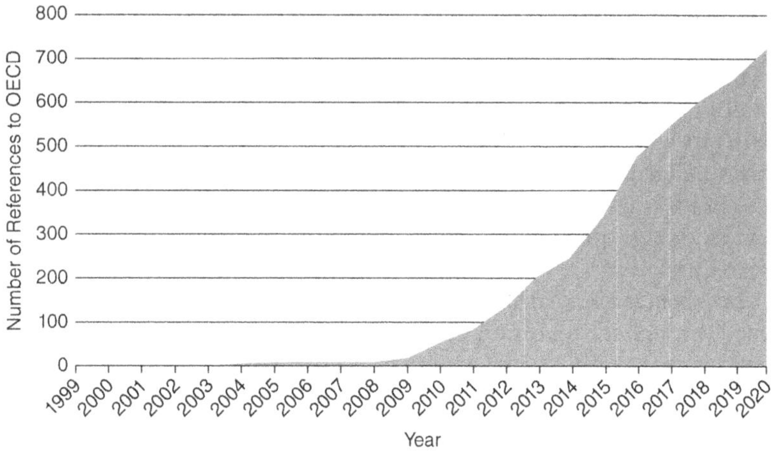

Figure 6.3 Cumulative references to the OECD in G20 summit and ministerial communiqués, 1999–2020

Source: Derived from G20 communiqués published by the University of Toronto G8 Information Centre, http://www.g20.utoronto.ca/summits/index.html, http://www.g20.utoronto.ca/ministerials.html, and http://www.g20.utoronto.ca/other.html.

most dynamic and systemically-important economies into the work of the OECD"[45] and the desire for its standards to resonate globally. By embroiling non-OECD G20 countries in its work the OECD can appease demands for greater inclusivity while avoiding the drawbacks of their membership. The G20's endorsement also legitimizes the OECD's agenda and contributes to the global acceptability of its standards.[46] According to Gurria, the OECD's "strategic engagement with the G20 and G7 has helped to globalize our standards in areas like taxes, competition, investment, anti-corruption, integrity, SME financing, state-owned enterprises, responsible business conduct, consumer policy, digital economy, and development finance."[47]

For the moment, opposition in both forums makes it unlikely that the OECD-G7/8/20 relationship will be consecrated. The G7/8/20's lean organizational model is consciously designed to liberate political leaders from the bureaucratization of international politics. Consequently, the G7/8/20 leaders have regularly repudiated plans to saddle the system with a permanent secretariat. Many OECD member states are already irritated by the organization's seeming subordination to forums from which they are excluded. With nine non-OECD members (Argentina, Brazil, China, the EU, India, Indonesia, Russia,

Saudi Arabia, and South Africa) the G20's intrusion onto the OECD agenda is particularly irksome. Assignments cascading down from the G20 bypass OECD decision making structures, disenfranchising members and skewing the organization's priorities toward outsiders. Reflecting this, the financial contributions of the Key Partners, although they remain peripheral overall, rose almost fivefold to €5.7 million in the decade to 2017.[48] Becoming a permanent G7/8/20 secretariat would also tie the OECD's fate to a group of institutions whose prospects are precarious. Latterly, the obstreperousness of the Trump administration has exacerbated perennial concerns about the G7/8/20's legitimacy and performance.[49] At a time when the OECD wants to parade its continued relevance and subdue indictments about its illegitimacy, members and staffers have reservations about becoming entangled with a G7/8/20 system that, at best, is seen as an irreverent "global hot tub party"[50] but, at worst, is regarded as a malign epicenter of global governance peddling policies that pander to the interests of an elite group of states while condemning a marginalized majority to impoverishment, instability and insecurity.

Conclusion: The battle for the OECD's soul

So far, the reforms under the rubric of the Global Relations Strategy are safeguarding the OECD's seat at the top table of global governance (see also Chapter 2). The enlargement process plus a litany of partnerships with non-member states is cementing the OECD's cooperation with a perpetually expanding cast of countries and actors. In turn, this is consolidating the OECD's position as the organization of choice to prepare and sustain cooperative activities in international institutions, most notably the G7/8 and G20, and whose standards shape the governance of a catalogue of leading issues (see Chapter 5).

Equally the indications are that the OECD is struggling to contain the contradictions inherent in the reform process. First, the OECD is walking the tightrope between inclusivity and ineffectiveness. While welcoming the dividends of legitimacy and dynamism, a survey of members in 2014 revealed a "general concern as to how the quality of OECD products and participation can be maintained with a more diverse and enlarged membership and, in particular, how the continued use of consensus could compromise the quality of outputs."[51] The tinkering with governance processes in which the OECD has indulged appear inadequate to deal with the looming sclerosis facing an organization whose membership has almost doubled since the end of the Cold War. Second, the OECD confronts a tradeoff between likemindedness, legitimacy, and effectiveness. The OECD clings to the mantra that it "need not be universal to be effective."[52] Nevertheless, until the Key Players are members, the OECD will be susceptible to the charge that it is not a legitimate forum in which to broker global rules. Similarly, the applicability and effectiveness of OECD standards may be undermined by the refusal of powerful non-members to acquiesce in rules they did not design. Incorporating the Key Players, however, would further diminish the prospects for consensus and risk contaminating the OECD's identity as a forum for market democracies.

As the incongruities of OECD reform mount, the momentum behind the process is dissipating. Already contentious, issues about the pace of enlargement, the traits of new members, and the procedural overhaul needed to finesse the transition have become further bogged down by deteriorating geopolitical circumstances. That it is proving difficult to get states to coalesce around a common vision for the organization is unsurprising. What is at stake is a battle for the very soul, and perhaps even the survival, of the OECD. It is to the OECD's future that our attention must now turn.

Notes

1 Daniel W. Drezner, *The System Worked: How the World Stopped another Great Depression* (Oxford: Oxford University Press, 2014).
2 Thomas Hale, David Held, and Kevin Young, *Gridlock: Why Global Cooperation is Failing When We Need It Most* (Cambridge: Polity, 2013).
3 Mark Blyth, *Austerity: The History of a Dangerous Idea* (Oxford: Oxford University Press, 2013).
4 Yvan Guillemette and David Turner, "The Long View: Scenarios for the World Economy to 2060," *OECD Economic Policy Papers* No. 22, https://www.oecd-ilibrary.org/deliver/b4f4e03e-en.pdf?itemId=%2Fcontent%2Fpaper%2Fb4f4e03e-en&mimeType=pdf.
5 Quoted in James Kanter, "When a Club of Winners Loses Its Way," *International Herald Tribune*, 10 February 2006.
6 OECD, *Making OECD Standards and Policies Count on a Global Scale*, C/MIN(2019)11, 7 May 2019, 3.
7 Judith Clifton and Daniel Diaz-Fuentes, "From 'Club of the Rich' to 'Globalisation a la carte'? Evaluating Reform at the OECD," *Global Policy* 2, no. 3 (2011): 300–11.
8 OECD, *2019 Strategic Orientations of the Secretary-General*, C/MIN (2019)1, 14 May 2019, 14.
9 ibid., 14.
10 OECD, *2016 Ministerial Council Statement "Enhancing Productivity for Inclusive Growth,"* C/MIN(2016)8/FINAL, 2 June 2016.
11 OECD, *Report of the Chair of the Working Group on the Future Size and Membership of the Organisation to Council. Framework for the Consideration of Prospective Members*, C(2017)50/FINAL, 5 June 2017, 4.

12 OECD, *A Strategy for Enlargement and Outreach: Report by the Chair of the Heads of Delegation Working Group on the Enlargement Strategy and Outreach, Ambassador Seiichiro Noburu* (Paris: OECD, 2004), 16–18.
13 OECD, *Resolution to Establish a Mechanism to Identify Countries for Potential Accession and Countries for Enhanced Engagement with the OECD*, C(2006)105/REV1, 13 July 2006.
14 OECD, *OECD's 50th Anniversary Vision Statement*, C/MIN(2011)6, 17 June 2006.
15 OECD, *The OECD's Global Relations: Report to the 2013 MCM*, C(2013)27/REV2, 24 April 2013.
16 OECD, *Report of the Chair of the Working Group on the Future Size and Membership of the Organisation to Council*, 7–17.
17 OECD, *OECD's 50th Anniversary Vision Statement*, 2.
18 IMF, *World Economic Outlook Database, April 2020*, https://www.imf.org/en/Publications/WEO/weo-database/2021/April.
19 See Aynsley Kellow and Peter Carroll, *Middle Powers and International Organizations: Australia and the OECD* (Cheltenham: Edward Elgar, 2017), 340.
20 OECD, *OECD Council Resolution on Enlargement and Enhanced Engagement*, C/MIN(2007)4/FINAL, 16 May 2007.
21 OECD, *A General Procedure for Future Accessions*, C(2007)31/FINAL, 16 May 2007, 4.
22 Confidential interview with senior OECD official, 18 June 2008.
23 OECD, *Resolutions of the Council on the Governance of the Organisation*, C(2015)100, 13 July 2015; OECD, *Council Working Group on Governance: Report on the Results of the Survey on Working Methods and Decision-Making of OECD Committees*, C/WGG(2014(1), 8 September 2014.
24 OECD, *2020 Strategic Orientations of the Secretary-General*, C(2020)31/REV2, 2 June 2020, 15.
25 Kishore Mahbubani, "The OECD: A Classic Sunset Organization," *Global Policy* 3, no. 1 (2012): 117.
26 OECD, *Revised Resolution of the Council on Partnership in OECD Bodies*, C(2012)100/REV1/FINAL, 4 December 2015.
27 OECD, *The OECD's Global Relations*, 27; OECD, *Guidelines to Committees for Deepening Enhanced Engagement*, C(2010)100/FINAL, 7 December 2010.
28 Judith Clifton and Daniel Diaz-Fuentes, "Is the Organisation for Economic Co-operation and Development Ready for China?," *Emerging Markets Finance and Trade* 50, no. 6 (2014): 30–33.
29 Magdalena Lachowicz, "Russia and the Prospect of OECD Membership: Between de jure and de facto Modernization," *Yearbook of the Institute of East-Central Europe* 14, no. 4 (2016): 153–60.
30 OECD, *Regional Approaches: Synthesis and Strategic Guidance*, C(2006)168/FINAL, 17 January 2007.
31 OECD, *Making OECD Standards and Policies Count on a Global Scale*, C/MIN(2020)4, 21 October 2020, 8.
32 OECD, *A Framework for the Establishment of Country Programmes*, C-MIN(2013)12, 30 April 2013.
33 OECD, *Review of the OECD Global Forums*, C(2007)131/FINAL.

34 OECD, *Making OECD Standards and Policies Count on a Global Scale*, 5–7.
35 Sieglinde Gstöhl, "Governance Through Government Networks: The G8 and International Organizations," *Review of International Organizations* 2, no. 1 (2007): 1–37.
36 OECD, *The OECD at Work* (Paris: OECD, 1964), 6.
37 Nicholas Bayne, *Hanging in There: The G7 and G8 Summit in Maturity and Renewal* (Aldershot: Ashgate, 2007), 8.
38 Donald Johnston, "Look no Further for a Home for Global Bodies," *Financial Times*, 28 November 2005, 13.
39 G20, "G20 Leaders Statement: The Pittsburgh Summit," http://www.g20.utoronto.ca/2009/2009communique0925.html.
40 Richard Eccleston, *The Dynamics of Global Economic Governance: The Financial Crisis, the OECD and the Politics of International Tax Cooperation* (Cheltenham: Edward Elgar, 2012), 86–91.
41 G20, "London Summit – Leaders' Statement 2 April 2009," http://www.g20.utoronto.ca/2009/2009communique0402.pdf.
42 Andrew F. Cooper, "The G20 as an Improvised Crisis Committee and/or a Contested 'Steering Committee' for the World," *International Affairs* 86, no. 3 (2010): 741–57.
43 Javier Solana, Angel Saz-Carranza and Enrique Rueda, *From G20 to Global Leadership: A Gap to be Filled*, 7 September 2020, https://dobetter.esade.edu/en/g20-global-leadership.
44 G. John Ikenberry, "Salvaging the G-7," *Foreign Affairs* 72, no. 2 (1993): 136–38.
45 OECD, *Resolution of the Council on Strengthening the OECD's Global Reach*, C(2013)58/FINAL, 30 May 2013, 2.
46 Richard Eccleston, Aynsley Kellow and Peter Carroll, "G20 Endorsement in Post Crisis Global Governance: More than a Toothless Talking Shop?," *British Journal of Politics and International Relations* 17, no. 2 (2015): 300.
47 OECD, *2019 Strategic Orientations of the Secretary-General*, 12.
48 OECD, *The OECD's Global Relations: Meeting the Strategic Challenges*, C/MIN(2018)8, 15 May 2018, 42–3.
49 Jakob Vestergaard, "The Future of Global Economic Governance: From the G20 to a Global Economic Council," http://www.institutdelors.eu/wp-content/uploads/2018/01/tgae20116gvestergaard.pdf; Jakob Vestergaard, *The G20 and Beyond: Towards Effective Global Economic Governance*, DIIS Report 2011:04, https://www.diis.dk/files/media/publications/import/extra/rp2011-04-g20-and-beyond_web_0.pdf.
50 John J. Kirton, *G20 Governance for a Globalized World* (Cheltenham: Ashgate, 2013), 38.
51 OECD, *Council Working Group on Governance*, 49.
52 OECD, *Report of the Chair of the Working Group on the Future Size and Membership of the Organisation to Council*, 3.

7 Conclusion: Into the sunset or out of the shadows? The future of the OECD

In June 2021, Mathias Cormann became Secretary-General of the OECD. Inheriting an in-tray overflowing with problems stemming from a global economy pummeled by the effects of the COVID-19 emergency, Cormann took the helm at a moment when the organization is, once again, at a crossroads. Those with a passing acquaintance with the OECD could be forgiven for concluding that it, along with the other constituent organizations of the LIEO, is in perennial disarray. The squabbling members, budgetary austerity, and indictments of illegitimacy and ineffectiveness that cloud the contemporary climate are recurrent themes in the histories of the international economic organizations. There is, nevertheless, a sentiment that this time is different with individual institutions, and perhaps even the liberal order itself, facing an existential moment.

This chapter cogitates about the OECD's future, offering three scenarios about its prospective role in global governance. The first scenario sees a senescent OECD sailing into the sunset, its death warrant signed by inexorable shifts in the global balance of power.[1] As US hegemony fades, the OECD will be consigned to history as the rules and institutions of the LIEO are steadily eclipsed by rivals embodying the ideas and interests of the rising powers. The second scenario is succession. According to this view, the rising powers lack the wherewithal, vision, or ambition to realize an alternative global order. Instead of a hegemonic transition, this perspective prophesizes the world going back to the future by fragmenting into coexisting spheres of influence representing contrasting value systems.[2] Just as they leavened the transition from the OEEC to the OECD, changing circumstances will see a replacement organization rising phoenix like from the ashes of its predecessor. The final scenario is more sanguine and envisages the OECD's survival as the rising powers are contained, albeit awkwardly and capriciously, within an evolving liberal order.[3]

DOI: 10.4324/9781351025867-8

Regardless of US decline, this standpoint believes the liberal order is difficult to depose because of the benefits it brings to the rising powers and its hardwiring into the routines of actors worldwide.[4] It is outlandish to suggest that the rising powers will be fully socialized into the OECD (see Chapter 6); equally the organization's bureaucratic assets and concomitant genius for adaptation will allow it to adjust to external environmental challenges, thereby sustaining its relevance to twenty-first century global governance.

Scenario one: Into the sunset

When in 1948 U.S. Congressional representatives insisted upon a permanent organization to oversee the Marshall Plan, few would have envisaged that these arrangements would endure for over 70 years, outliving, and eventually absorbing, some of their communist foes to become a cornerstone of the LIEO. As Chapter 1 discussed, the OEEC and OECD were incubated in the womb of US hegemony as part of a liberal order "organized around economic openness, multilateral institutions, security cooperation and democratic solidarity."[5] Reflecting Cold War realities, participation in the liberal order was confined initially to the Western bloc. Through Western dominated organizations such as the IMF and GATT and exclusively Western organizations like the OEEC and OECD, the countries of the free world nursed the international order through its infancy, conceiving rules, norms, and principles to guide, within clear limits, the liberalization of their economies. This system of embedded liberalism, "involving a new commitment to a form of institutionalized liberal multilateralism that was compatible with various kinds of active public management of the economy,"[6] aimed to enable members to reap the benefits of cross-border commerce whilst retaining sufficient autonomy to inoculate citizens against any resultant economic instability. Over the next four decades, the parents of the international order doted on their offspring screening it against infection (such as excessive trade protectionism), taming its teenage tantrums (such as the oil crisis), and imbuing it with suitable values for adulthood (market democracy). The international order's coming of age arrived with the collapse of the Soviet bloc whereupon the United States, egged on by its allies, embarked on a project to globalize the Western model. For commentators beholden to our first scenario, however, this moment of hegemonic hubris precipitated processes likely to have fatal consequences for the LIEO and the OECD's place in global governance.

Believing that the destiny of the post-1945 international order is intimately intertwined with that of US hegemony, subscribers to this view worry that the changes catalyzed by the globalization of the liberal order are undermining the ability and willingness of the United States to discharge this role. Buoyed by their Cold War triumph and overweening declarations of the "end of history,"[7] the Western powers set about exporting capitalism to the rest of the world, believing that through their integration into global markets countries would inevitably develop a need for the rule of law and representative democracy thus sealing their peaceful rise within the existing order. Instead, by turbocharging growth in the so-called BRICS and N11[8] countries, their assimilation into the global economy has triggered tectonic changes in the structure of global power. The relentless "rise of the rest,"[9] most notably China, heralds the extinction of US hegemony. States which prior to their economic rise were rule takers that meekly acquiesced in the rituals of the LIEO now have ambitions to be rule makers challenging the status quo by waging campaigns to radically overhaul existing bodies or to found new institutions that better embody their interests.

Given its genius for "organizational adaptation,"[10] it might be argued that the OECD should not be unduly perturbed. For champions of the liberal order, the "goal should be to reconfigure rights and responsibilities in existing institutions to reflect the diffusion of power in an increasingly multipolar world."[11] As the deadlocks beleaguering attempts to reform the other multilateral economic institutions demonstrate[12], however, this is not easily realized. For the OECD, the difficulties are compounded by the exclusion of the rising powers from its membership. If the process of reform is fraying the fabric of the OECD (see Chapter 6), the incorporation of the BRICS promises to rupture it beyond repair. To date, the OECD has handled this dilemma through a smorgasbord of partnerships with non-members. Given current trends in global economic geography, this strategy looks unsustainable, not least as it will exacerbate the OECD's vulnerability to forum shopping. Given the absence of many systemically important countries, OECD members may conclude that they need to look elsewhere to deliver workable solutions to the most pressing problems of global governance. Besides, if emerging powers are set on altering the prevailing norms of global governance, they are less likely to countenance the OECD's use as a pre-negotiating or preparatory forum (see Chapter 4) that paves the way to more formal agreements in other venues.

Elsewhere narratives prophesying the deterioration of US power have been questioned. Like the previous waves of 'declinist' sentiment that have washed over the debate on US hegemony, the current jeremiads stand accused of embellishing the potency of America's rivals or underestimating that of the United States. These observers point to overwhelming military superiority, the use of the dollar as an international reserve currency, a vast "non-territorial empire"[13] of American controlled multinational enterprises, and deep reserves of soft power ensuring the United States' immediate, if not indefinite,[14] preeminence. For many of these commentators, the threat to the liberal order comes not from diminished US power, but the United States' abdication of its global leadership role.[15] Again, these developments are traceable to decisions perpetuated since the 1990s, which have decimated domestic consent for the liberal order among its key patrons.[16] Jettisoning the embedded liberal pact, international organizations such as the OECD exuded a newfound enthusiasm for the neoliberal model (see Chapter 2). This paradigm posited that the route to economic nirvana lay in minimizing barriers to trade and investment. Unfortunately, the benefits of competitiveness and prosperity bypassed many American citizens and their counterparts in other industrial societies. For them the exposure to global market forces has meant stagnant wages, the offshoring of manufacturing jobs, precarious employment, rising income inequality, and economic insecurity. Tapping into this well of discontent, Donald Trump came to power by promising to bring to heel the "globalists" that had hoodwinked the United States into bankrolling an international order that inflicted "carnage"[17] upon American society.[18]

Trump's term of office caused immense harm to the United States' international leadership credentials. During this time, the President regularly inveighed against multilateral institutions and headed an administration that reneged on international accords such as the Paris Agreement and the Transpacific Partnership, quit UNESCO and the WHO, equivocated about the United States' commitment to NATO's principle of mutual defense, sabotaged the WTO's dispute settlement mechanism, and outlined a vision of global governance based not on the rules-based order of the past but ad hoc cooperation among "strong and independent nations that embrace their sovereignty."[19] Labeled the "withdrawal doctrine,"[20] these actions have tallied with harmful inaction deriving from decisions deliberately designed to debilitate the United States' diplomatic capability.[21] Unlike many international organizations, the OECD was spared a full-frontal fusillade from Trump's rhetorical bazooka. It would nonetheless be a mistake to infer that the OECD has escaped unscathed. Echoing the United States' wider disengagement, the administration took almost four years to gain approval for a Permanent Representative to the OECD and, although scotched by Congress, repeatedly proposed defunding the OECD as a body whose results and hence contribution to US interests is unclear.[22] Deprived of the hegemonic sinews needed to cajole or coerce increasingly fractious members into collective action, cooperation in the OECD is seizing up.[23]

Thus, whether through decline or disinterest, the end of American hegemony means the OECD is entering a self-fulfilling cycle of decline. With members seeing less value in multilateralism and non-members "routing around"[24] an organization which they perceive as hostile to their interests, the OECD's status and budget will shrivel. The demoralizing effect on staff will prompt skilled personnel to leave, denuding the OECD of the expertise so essential to its comparative advantage. Progressively marginalized from the paramount issues of global governance, the OECD will drift into obscurity.

Scenario two: Phoenix from the flames

The United States may no longer possess the inclination or the collateral to assume the mantle of global hegemon but neither, for the moment, do its rivals. China, its most plausible replacement, remains a "reluctant power"[25] whose leaders, wary of direct confrontation with the United States, the constraints international institutions would place upon their actions, and the costs of bankrolling military alliances and adventures, regularly repudiate reports that they aspire to global supremacy. China mostly exerts its power subtly by pressing for reform of, and acquiring more prominent positions in, existing institutions. That said, there is evidence of China adopting a more muscular approach and resorting to the creation of parallel institutions, most notably the Asian Infrastructure Investment Bank (AIIB), when its interests are ignored. Likewise, capitalizing on the vacuum left by the United States, China, and other rising powers are becoming more assertive in their regional backyards.[26] Based on this budding bipolar or multipolar configuration of global power, the second scenario eyes the world order splintering into blocs governed by competing ideologies and institutions. In turn, this may rejuvenate interest in an OECD-like body as the hub of a bounded order of market democracies.

That the investiture of the AIIB was greeted with such fanfare reflected a widespread perception that it signified a milestone in the history of global economic governance. Specifically, it was interpreted as the opening salvo in the articulation by rising powers of a parallel system predicated on institutional arrangements and modes of governance distinct from those prevailing in the LIEO. Talk of a coherent "China model"[27] or "Beijing consensus"[28] may be premature but the contours of a Chinese led order, grounded in state-capitalism and authoritarianism, are discernible. The delivery of domestic political stability, explosive economic growth, plunging poverty rates, and globally competitive firms is winning the Chinese blueprint admirers and establishing it as a viable alternative to market democracy as a formula to promote human development. Additionally, through the AIIB and the much broader Belt and Road Initiative, China is using its financial firepower to seduce others into emulating its path to modernity. By remaking countries in its image and tying their economic well-being to its fortunes, China hopes to make them more receptive to its overtures and susceptible to recruitment into its sphere of influence.

Faced with a potential axis of authoritarianism calls for a counterweight correlation of forces, variously christened the "coalition of the responsible,"[29] "concert of democracies,"[30] Group of 9,[31] and Democracies 10 (D10),[32] are proliferating. These proposals are finding favor in many OECD capitals. For instance, in July 2020, the US Secretary of State mused "maybe it's time for a new grouping of like-minded nations, a new alliance of democracies."[33] By seizing upon this groundswell of opinion an entrepreneurial Secretary-General could champion the credentials of the OECD, a self-styled club of market democracies, to contribute to this mission. Although it is diminishing (see Table 2.1), the OECD forecasts that by 2060 its current members will still account for 49 percent of global nominal GDP (42 percent in PPP terms).[34] The OECD will therefore remain a formidable faction in any discussions about the future governance of the global economy. The OECD can also point to a successful track record in helping to face down an ideological foe (see Chapter 2).

To be a serious contender to play this role will almost certainly necessitate reforms to the OECD, for example, to the membership and decision-making apparatus, that members have previously been unable to stomach. The present geopolitical juncture may not only help to overcome the impasse in the OECD reform process (see Chapter 6) but also provide the impetus for an overhaul so drastic that its effects cannot be accommodated within the OECD's present structure. In other words, just as the redrawing of the world's geopolitical battle lines once convinced states to back the metamorphosis of a faltering OEEC into the OECD, so the present circumstances may entice them to support another evolution. Rallying likeminded countries around a grand bargain for a successor organization would almost certainly rely on the wherewithal of the United States. China's continued rise as a strategic competitor may be the jolt needed for the United States to conquer its aversion to international leadership and spark its interest in more selective institutional settings.[35] In many universal multilateral organizations, international cooperation has come to a standstill owing to the divergent preferences of the United States and the rising powers, a problem exacerbated by power shifts that have left the former unwilling or unable to impose its will on the latter. Just as it has done in the past (see Chapter 1), the United States might choose to circumvent these problems by channeling cooperative ventures through more exclusive institutions of likeminded partners. Exploiting the anxieties around rising powers, the United States can use its position as first among equals to attain better burden sharing with its allies, something it has long craved.[36]

The route to a new organization would remain rocky, however. Faced with a power grab by the OECD other organizations, fearful of their own fate, and their supporters are unlikely to stand idly by. NATO, for example, could claim that it provides a firmer foundation for a club of democracies, especially given the security implications of the unfolding international environment.[37] Awkward questions about membership would also resurface. For instance, would the current membership be grandfathered into the successor organization and who else would be eligible to join? The growing economic dependence of many countries on China may also hinder moves toward a repurposed OECD. To avoid antagonizing the Chinese, prospective members may be reluctant to join such an organization. Indeed, existing OECD members, especially Asian and Latin American countries with closer economic ties to China, may prefer the current arrangements which allow them to maintain more equidistant relationships between the West and "the rest."

Scenario three: Survival

The final scenario holds that irrespective of the geopolitical upheavals seemingly underway, the LIEO "can remain the dominating logic of the twenty-first century."[38] The LIEO is cleverly designed so that while it structures the world in a way that benefits the United States it also commands loyalty by bringing advantages to others. Likewise, it is "easy to join,"[39] something that has enabled the integration of the rising powers who are now among the LIEO's chief beneficiaries. Far from seeking its overthrow, rising powers are looking to advance their interests by manipulating the LIEO and obtaining a louder voice in its institutions.[40] In other words, proponents of this view believe that the rising powers will be effectively contained within the LIEO. Even if the United States is no longer willing or able to lead, it is in the interests of prominent states to pick up the slack thereby ensuring that the institutions of international economic cooperation will survive "after hegemony."[41]

The lengthy list of problems besieging humanity twinned with the recognition that they cannot be solved by states acting in isolation will sustain interest in multilateralism. Environmental degradation, widespread poverty, recurrent financial crisis, and the COVID-19 pandemic starkly illustrate the flaws of the present system of global governance. For all their fulmination against global institutions, states are strongly inclined to pursue their interests through them. As the previous Secretary-General observed, "the services and support of the OECD are more requested than ever before while, paradoxically, multilateralism is being questioned."[42] Indeed, its imperfections notwithstanding, there are several facets of the OECD's institutional personality which give grounds for optimism about its survival in the global governance architecture.[43]

First, the nebulous nature of its mission imbues the OECD with the latitude to cope with the vicissitudes of global politics. The OECD is adept at venturing into new areas or repurposing existing mandates in response to the whims of states. These "chameleon-like"[44] qualities keep the OECD at the crux of a multitude of cutting-edge issues including AI, blockchain, climate change, tax transparency, and sustainable development (see Chapter 5). The OECD's all-encompassing remit also means that logjams in one policy domain do not prevent progress in others, empowering the organization to continue delivering relevant outputs despite the diverging preferences of its paymasters.

Second, in warding off external pressures, another weapon in the OECD's armory is the size, scope, and savvy of the Secretariat. As Chapters 3 and 4 documented, through the competences and resources delegated to the Secretariat by member states and the authority deriving from its accumulated policy expertise, OECD officials can influence, within limits, the trajectory of the organization. Any imminent prospect of dissolution would incentivize officials to remind states of the OECD's role in advancing their interests. To this end, officials will redouble their efforts to make headway on projects by brokering compromises between states and advertising the OECD's virtues as a venue for future cooperative ventures. When tendering for this work, the nature of the Secretariat confers the OECD with certain comparative advantages. Few, if any, other organizations can match the depth and breadth of the OECD's economic expertise. On many topics, the OECD's institutional memory dates to its foundation (and in some cases predates it) giving the organization an unsurpassed repository of accumulated knowledge and experience on which to draw. Similarly, when policy challenges emerge, the OECD is invariably blessed with preexisting expertise. As Chapter 4 noted, the OECD is dexterous at defining emerging policy challenges. By building narratives around these issues and inventing the language and concepts needed to comprehend them, the Secretariat shapes the preferences of states, convincing them not only of their interest in solving these problems but also that the OECD is the natural home to pursue it. The organization's propensity for carving out such niches is bolstered by the range of subjects the OECD bestrides. Given the multidimensional nature of most policy conundrums, the OECD's readiness to liberate specialists from their disciplinary silos is particularly prized. This interdisciplinary tradition, exemplified in the past by projects such as the "problems of modern society" (see Chapter 1) and today by NAEC (see Chapters 2 and 5), permits the OECD to establish and explore linkages between topics that are compartmentalized elsewhere.

Third, whereas the changing global power landscape militates against it, the techniques and temperament of global economic governance are converging with those of the OECD. For example, in the twenty-first century, there has been a trend toward the informalization of global economic governance marked by a shift away from legally codified and binding agreements toward "loose arrangements, common understandings, implicit rules, flexibility, and pragmatism."[45] Anticipating that soft law and soft power will be the "means to success in world politics,"[46] the OECD is sometimes envisaged as the archetype for future international institutions.[47] Furthermore, while the intensified institutional density of global governance means extra competition for the OECD it also unlocks complementarities. Recent decades have witnessed a proliferation of organizational forms incorporating informal clubs such as the "G-groups," transgovernmental networks and private transnational organizations of actors from civil society and business.[48] These bodies lack some or all the paraphernalia associated with international organizations such as a headquarters, formal rules and decision-making procedures and a supporting bureaucracy. Free of such encumbrances they tend to be nimbler and cheaper but equally suffer shortfalls in resources and expertise. Because it positions itself upstream and downstream of these institutions, resolving gridlocks prior to their meetings and nudging work forward in their aftermath, the OECD will remain critical to the ecology of global governance.

Conclusion

In the short-term, the OECD is almost certain to muddle through. The OECD exhibits several characteristics which, as institutional theorists have observed, allow international organizations to adapt to changing external surroundings including the ambiguity in its mandate, penchant for consensus decision making and ample Secretariat.[49] The OECD's longevity and organizational assets also represent considerable investments by member states. For institutionalists, it is paradoxically the "sunk" nature of these costs that help keep international organizations afloat.[50] In any case, the continued clamor for membership and the absence of threats to secede suggest that states still perceive benefits arising from OECD membership. The context of COVID-19 has reinforced messages about the OECD's value. Although primarily a healthcare crisis, COVID-19 is simultaneously an economic, educational, environmental, fiscal, developmental, humanitarian, and social crisis. As such, the pandemic is a timely reminder of the fiendish complexity of twenty-first century challenges, such as climate change, and the richness of the OECD's expertise which, among the international economic organizations, leave it uniquely poised to "engage in this deep, multi-disciplinary, whole of government reflection of the changes needed in our economic systems."[51]

Long-term salvation, however, lies in member states first finding a compelling and collective answer to the question that has bedeviled the organization from the outset namely, what is the OECD for? Churlish as it may be to complain about an organization that is devoted to helping governments to detect solutions to common problems, as one of the very first essays on the OEEC/OECD remarked "there must be a real purpose to be served, and not merely a romantic desire for cooperation."[52] Beyond this, the members must resolve questions about the OECD's relationship with non-members and, by extension, its positioning in the architecture of global governance. With the OECD's present approach seemingly running out of road and changes in global power structures abbreviating the tarmac further, alternative thoroughfares are needed. This will nonetheless be a delicate operation, with all the most obvious routes to redemption involving unpalatable trade-offs. As two distinguished liberal international relations scholars have argued, "liberalism has a pragmatic adaptability and a penchant for institutional innovations that are vital for responding to.......emerging challenges."[53] In other words, whether the OECD can overcome these challenges is perhaps the ultimate test of the values it champions. The stakes could not be higher.

If it succeeds, the OECD will persist as a significant, if spectral, presence in global governance. If not, the latest Secretary-General of the OECD could well be its last.

Notes

1 Kishore Mahbubani, "The OECD: A Classic Sunset Organisation," *Global Policy* 3, no. 1 (2012): 117–18.
2 John J. Mearsheimer, "Bound to Fail: The Rise and Fall of the Liberal International Order," *International Security* 43, no. 4 (2019): 7–50.
3 Nana de Graaff, Tobias ten Brink and Inderjeet Parmar, "China's Rise in a Liberal World Order in Transition – Introduction to the FORUM," *Review of International Political Economy* 27, no. 2 (2020): 194–97.
4 G. John Ikenberry, *Liberal Leviathan: The Origins, Crisis, and Transformation of the American World Order* (Princeton, N.J.: Princeton University Press, 2011).
5 G. John Ikenberry, "The End of the Liberal International Order?," *International Affairs* 94, no. 1 (2018): 7.
6 Eric Helleiner, "The Life and Times of Embedded Liberalism: Legacies and Innovations Since Bretton Woods," *Review of International Political Economy* 26, no. 6 (2019): 1113.
7 Francis Fukuyama, *The End of History and the Last Man* (London: Penguin, 1992).
8 On the N11, see Jim O'Neill, "The 'Next Eleven' and the World Economy," https://www.project-syndicate.org/commentary/n-11-global-economy-by-jim-o-neill-2018-04.
9 Fareed Zakaria, *The Post-American World: And the Rise of the Rest* (London: Penguin, 2009).
10 Peter Carroll and Aynsley Kellow, *The OECD: A Study of Organisational Adaptation* (Cheltenham: Edward Elgar, 2011).
11 Ikenberry, "The End of the Liberal International Order?," 22.
12 Edwin M. Truman, "IMF Quota and Governance Reform Once Again," *Peterson Institute for International Economics Policy Brief* 18–9, 2018, https://www.piie.com/system/files/documents/pb18-9.pdf.
13 Susan Strange, "The Future of the American Empire," *Journal of International Affairs* 42, no. 1 (1988): 6.
14 Michael Beckley, "China's Century? Why America's edge will Endure," *International Security* 36, no. 3 (2011-12): 41–78.
15 Richard Haass, *A World in Disarray: American Foreign Policy and the Crisis of the Old Order* (New York: Penguin, 2018): 309-28; Ivo Daalder and James M. Lindsay, *The Empty Throne: America's Abdication of Global Leadership* (New York: Public Affairs, 2018); Robert Kagan, *The Jungle Grows Back: America and Our Imperilled World* (New York: Vintage Books, 2019).
16 Doug Stokes, "Trump, American Hegemony and the Future of the Liberal International Order," *International Affairs* 94, no. 1 (2018): 145–49.
17 Donald J. Trump, "Remarks of President Donald J. Trump – As Prepared for Delivery Inaugural Address," 20 January 2017, https://www.whitehouse.gov/briefings-statements/the-inaugural-address/.

18 Christopher Layne, "The US-Chinese Power Shift at the End of the Pax Americana," *International Affairs* 94, no. 1 (2018): 89–111.

19 UN, "Statement by H.E. Mr. Donald Trump President of the United States of America at the Seventy-Second Regular Session of the United Nations General Assembly," 19 September 2017, https://gadebate.un.org/sites/default/files/gastatements/72/us_en.pdf.

20 Richard N. Haass, "Trump's Foreign Policy Doctrine? The Withdrawal Doctrine," *Washington Post* 27 May 2020, https://www.washingtonpost.com/opinions/2020/05/27/trumps-foreign-policy-doctrine-withdrawal-doctrine/; Richard N. Haass, "Present at the Disruption: How Trump Unmade U.S. Foreign Policy," *Foreign Affairs* 99, no. 5 (2020): 24–34.

21 Economist, "The Dereliction of American Diplomacy," *Economist* 436, no. 9207 (15-21 August 2020): 52–4.

22 US Congressional Research Service, *Department of State, Foreign Operations, and Related Programs: FY2021 Budget and Appropriations*, https://www.state.gov/wp-content/uploads/2020/02/FY-2021-CBJ-Final.pdf: 10. See also US Department of State, *Congressional Budget Justification: Department of State, Foreign Operations, and Related Programs*, https://www.state.gov/wp-content/uploads/2019/05/FY-2020-CBJ-FINAL.pdf: 40.

23 OECD, *2020 Strategic Orientations of the Secretary-General*, C(2020)31/REV2, 2 June 2020, 9.

24 Nazneen Barma, Ely Ratner and Steven Weber, "A World Without the West," *The National Interest* 90 (2007): 23-30; Alexander Cooley and Daniel H. Nexon, "How Hegemony Ends: The Unravelling of American Power," *Foreign Affairs* 99, no. 4 (2020): 147–51.

25 Evan A. Feigenbaum, "China and the World: Dealing With a Reluctant Power," *Foreign Affairs* 96, no. 1 (2017): 33–40.

26 Oriana S. Mastro, "The Stealth Superpower: How China Hid Its Global Ambitions," *Foreign Affairs* 98, no. 1 (2019): 31–9.

27 Joshua Kurlantzick, *Democracy in Retreat: The Revolt of the Middle Class and the Worldwide Decline of Representative Government* (New Haven, C.T.: Yale University Press, 2014), Chapter 7.

28 John Williamson, "Is the "Beijing Consensus" Now Dominant?," *Asia Policy* 13 (2012): 1–16.

29 Michael Fullilove, "After the Midterms: Australia, the United States and the International Order," 13 November 2018 https://www.lowyinstitute.org/publications/after-midterms-australia-united-states-and-international-order.

30 Ivo H. Daalder and James M. Lindsay, "Democracies of the World, Unite," *The American Interest* 2, no. 3 (2007): 5–15.

31 Ivo H. Daalder and James M. Lindsay, "The Committee to Save the World Order: America's Allies Must Step Up as America Steps Down," *Foreign Affairs* 97, no. 6 (2018): 72–83.

32 Ash Jain, *Like-Minded and Capable Democracies: A New Framework for Advancing a Liberal World Order*, Council on Foreign Relations International Institutions and Global Governance Program Working Paper 12, https://cdn.cfr.org/sites/default/files/pdf/2012/11/IIGG_WorkingPaper12_Jain.pdf.

33 Michael R. Pompeo, "Communist China and the Free World's Future," Speech by the Secretary of State The Richard Nixon Presidential

Library and Museum, Yorba Linda California, 23 July 2020, https://www.state.gov/communist-china-and-the-free-worlds-future/.

34 OECD, Long Term Growth Scenarios, *OECD Economics Department Working Papers No. 1000* ECO/WKP(2012)77, 28 January 2013: 32, 36.

35 Lora Anna Viola, "US Strategies of Institutional Adaptation in the Face of Hegemonic Decline," *Global Policy* 11, no. S3 (2020): 28–39.

36 Graham Allison, "The New Spheres of Influence: Sharing the Globe With Other Great Powers," *Foreign Affairs* 99, no. 2 (2020): 37–40.

37 Ivo Daalder and James Goldgeier, "Global NATO," *Foreign Affairs* 85, no. 5 (2006): 105–13.

38 G. John Ikenberry, *Liberal Leviathan: The Origins, Crisis, and Transformation of the American World Order,* 349.

39 G. John Ikenberry, "The Rise of China and the Future of the West: Can the Liberal System Survive?," *Foreign Affairs* 87, no. 1 (2008): 24.

40 G. John Ikenberry, "The Illusion of Geopolitics: The Enduring Power of the Liberal Order," *Foreign Affairs* 93, no. 3 (2014): 89.

41 Robert O. Keohane, *After Hegemony: Cooperation and Discord in the World Political Economy* (Princeton, N.J.: Princeton University Press, 1984).

42 OECD, *2019 Strategic Orientations of the Secretary-General,* CMIN(2019)1, 14 May 2019, 15.

43 See Maria Debre and Hylke Dijkstra, "Institutional Design for a Post-liberal Order: Why Some International Organizations Live Longer Then Others," *European Journal of International Relations*, forthcoming, https://journals.sagepub.com/doi/full/10.1177/1354066120962183.

44 Richard Woodward, "The Organisation for Economic Cooperation and Development," *New Political Economy* 9, no. 1 (2004): 121.

45 Matthew D. Stephen, "Emerging Powers and Emerging Trends in Global Governance," *Global Governance* 23, no. 3 (2017): 495.

46 Joseph S. Nye, *Soft Power: The Means to Success in World Politics* (New York: Public Affairs, 2004).

47 Anne-Marie Slaughter, "The Real New World Order," *Foreign Affairs* 76, no. 5 (1997): 196.

48 See Kenneth W. Abbott, Jessica F. Green and Robert O. Keohane, "Organizational Ecology and Institutional Change in Global Governance," *International Organization* 70, no. 2 (2016): 247–77.

49 Barbara Koremenos, "Loosening the Ties That Bind: A Learning Model of Agreement Flexibility," *International Organization* 55, no. 2 (2001): 289–325; Thomas Hale, David Held and Kevin Young, *Gridlock: Why Global Cooperation is Failing When We Need it Most* (Cambridge: Policy, 2013); Michael N. Barnett and Martha Finnemore, *Rules for the World: International Organizations in Global Politics* (Ithaca, N.Y.: Cornell University Press, 2004).

50 Keohane, *After Hegemony*, 102.

51 OECD, *2020 Strategic Orientations of the Secretary-General*, 9.

52 Lincoln Gordon, "The Organization for European Economic Cooperation," *International Organization* 10, no. 1 (1956): 11.

53 Daniel Deudney and G. John Ikenberry, "Liberal World: The Resilient Order," *Foreign Affairs* 97, no. 4 (2018): 17.

Select bibliography and electronic resources

General works on the OECD - organizational features, history, evolution

Matthieu Leimgruber and Matthias Schmelzer, ed. *The OECD and the International Political Economy Since 1948* (Basingstoke: Palgrave, 2017).
Wide-ranging historical analysis of the OECD and its role at critical junctures in the postwar economic story.
Peter Carroll and Aynsley Kellow, *The OECD: A Study of Organisational Adaptation* (Cheltenham: Edward Elgar, 2011).
Based on extensive archival research, narrates the first 50 years of the OECD story.
Peter Carroll and Aynsley Kellow, *The OECD From 2011-2021: A Decade of Transformation* (Berlin: De Gruyter, 2021).
Examines the OECD's evolution under Angel Gurria.
Lincoln Gordon, "The Organization for European Economic Cooperation," *International Organization* 10, no. 1 (1956): 1–11.
Miriam Camps, *"First World" Relationships: the role of the OECD* (Paris: The Atlantic Institute for International Affairs, 1975).
Two former US State Department employees who were intimately involved with the Marshall Plan reflect on the emergence and evolution of the OEEC/OECD and their role in sponsoring and managing Western interdependence.

Understanding the OECD's influence in global governance

David Howarth and Tal Sadeh, "In the vanguard of globalization: The OECD and international capital liberalization," *Review of International Political Economy* 18, no. 5 (2011): 622–45.
Paul Cammack, "The OECD and the world market: antecedents of deep marketization," *Globalizations* 19, no. 6 (2019): 804–18.
Two articles documenting the OECD's promotion of liberalization, marketization and globalization.

Judith Clifton and Daniel Diaz-Fuentes, "The OECD and phases in the international political economy, 1961-2011," *Review of International Political Economy* 18, no. 5 (2011): 552–69.

Probes the relationship between the OECD, the development of the post-war global economy and the theoretical literature on International Political Economy.

Richard Eccleston, *The Dynamics of Global Economic Governance: The Financial Crisis, the OECD and the Politics of International Tax Cooperation* (Cheltenham: Edward Elgar, 2013).

Examines, from various theoretical perspectives, the OECD's role in catalyzing and sustaining international cooperation in the field of taxation.

Kerstin Martens and Anja P. Jakobi, eds., *Mechanisms of OECD Governance: International Incentives for National Policy Making* (Oxford: Oxford University Press, 2010).

Identifies the impact of OECD ideas, data, standards, and evaluations on national level policymaking.

Matthias Schmelzer, *The Hegemony of Growth: The OECD and the making of the economic growth paradigm* (Cambridge: Cambridge University Press, 2016).

Investigates how the OEEC and OECD defined and redefined the meaning of economic growth and established it as a central public policy goal.

OECD work on contemporary issues

The *OECD Annual Report* and the *Key Information* booklet produced to support the Ministerial Council Meeting précis recent OECD activity. These are available from the OECD website (see below).

Peter Carroll and Adrian Kay, *Global Health Governance and the OECD* (Singapore: World Scientific Publishing, 2018).

Analysis of the rapid rise of health on the OECD agenda.

Xavier Pons, "Fifteen years of research on PISA effects on education governance: A critical review," *European Journal of Education* 52, no. 2 (2017): 131–44.

Dennis Niemann and Kerstin Martens, "Soft governance by hard fact? The OECD as a knowledge broker in education policy," *Global Social Policy* 18, no. 3 (2018): 267–83.

Two reviews demonstrating the impact of the OECD's knowledge, monitoring and research on global education policy.

The future of the OECD

OECD, *Report of the Chair of the Working Group on the Future Size and Membership of the Organization to the Council. Framework for the Consideration of the Prospective Members*, C(2017)50/FINAL, 5 June 2017.

OECD, *The OECD's Global Relations: Meeting the Strategic Challenges*, C/MIN(2018)8, 15 May 2018.

OECD, *Making OECD Standards and Policies Count on a Global Scale*, C/MIN(2019)11, 7 May 2019.

OECD, *2020 Strategic Orientations of the Secretary-General*, C(2020)31/REV2, 2 June 2020.

Electronic resources

www.oecd.org
The OECD's main website, available in English and French.
oecdobserver.org
In-house magazine providing commentary on contemporary issues of relevance to the organization and its members.
www.oecd-ilibrary.org
The OECD's online library featuring its books, papers, and statistical databases.
www.ru.nl/fm/iobio
Engaging pen portraits of the OECD Secretary-Generals.

Index

Made in the USA
Monee, IL
11 July 2026

56922598R10098